Bruges, Belgium.

Trip, Ecological Study

Author
James Baker.

Publisher:
SONIT
2162 Davenport House, 261 Bolton Road. Bury. Lancashire. BL8 2NZ. United Kingdom.

Table of Content

Summary

Traveling

There are many ways of spending free time. One of them is travelling. Certainly, it has its pros and cons.

First advantage of travelling is visiting interesting places and meeting new people. It is connected with getting to know other cultures and traditions which is surely valuable. Secondly, it is usually said that journeys educate, so whilst travelling as well as exploration we can make our knowledge wider. Also we become more experienced and ready to cope with surrounding world if we learn something while being in journey. Furthermore, travelling is the best solution for those of us who suffer from boredom or want to get away from ? grey reality? and experience great adventure. Journeys give to people a little fun and also make dreams come true.

On the other hand, journeys has some crucial disadvantages. Firstly, costs of travelling are often quiet high for example travelling by plane, so naturally not everyone can afford. What is more, journeys especially foreign ones expose us to danger of disease or even death. Travelling can lead to fall ill and maybe then to expensive treatment or in case of fatal accident like for instance car and aerial one to death of many people. The next disadvantage is fatigue that occur while travelling. Most journeys last very long and it can make us feel tired.

To sum up, travelling is a very good way of spending time. It can educate, give impressions, nice memories and let make friends. However, in my opinion travelling in spite of its whole advantages, it should not be the only way to learn about the world

Introduction

Bruges is a city that could have sprung from the pages of a Gothic fairy tale. Its cobbled streets, spidery canals, and medieval churches are remarkably well preserved, having been spared the devastation that saw much of Belgium leveled during the 20th-century wars. The secret got out years ago, though, and avoiding weekends and high season is often the only way to skirt the crowds that flood its many boutique hotels.

Indeed, tourism has long been the principal industry here, and preservation orders and strict bylaws ensure that the center looks much as it did during its medieval pomp (how the modern and modern-looking Concertgebouw Bruges concert venue on 't Zand got planning permission is still a matter of heated debate).

Today, the center is encircled by a ring road that loosely follows the line of the city's medieval ramparts. The ancient gates Smedenpoort, Ezelpoort, Kruispoort, and Gentpoort still stand along this route, and due to the city's size, all of its best sights, such as the impressive basilica or the Groeningemuseum, home to some of the finest paintings by Belgium's famed Flemish Primitive artists, can easily be reached on foot.

In modern times, Bruges has developed a reputation for culinary indulgence. More than 50 chocolate shops cram its narrow streets; there's even a museum dedicated to the history of cacao, while local artisans such as The Chocolate

Line's Dominique Persoone have gained international recognition. At the time of writing, Bruges also boasted as many three-starred Michelin restaurants as London. True, prices tend to be on the high side, but there are literally hundreds of places to dine, with some excellent seafood and traditional Belgian cuisine to be found across the city.

For many, though, beer is the main draw, with a number of Bruges's bars and estaminets considered among the finest around by connoisseurs. The city once housed nearly 60 breweries in its heyday, though today only a few remain—look out for local Fort Lapin, Straffe Hendrik, and Brugse Zot beers. For other beer-related activities, head to the Bruges Beer Museum or for a brewery tour at De Halve Maan

In truth, though, little changes in Bruges. It's a city that has been both liberated and constricted by its tourist appeal, and, like its famed chocolate, it is best sampled in small doses preferably one or two nights at the most. However, when the day-trippers head home and the shadows draw in, the wonderfully eerie, Gothic charm of this remarkable city emerges. To stroll its cobbled byways is to be transported back in time, and while you'll never have them all to yourself during the day, it really is one of the most atmospheric places in Europe.

Although it's often called Bruges (its French name) in many guidebooks (like this one) and by English-speakers, the city's official Flemish name is indeed Brugge (*bruhg-guh*), the spelling you'll see and hear most often while exploring the city.

History

In medieval times the sea flooded the area around present-day Bruges, carving out channels and waterways. Baldwin the Iron Arm, the first count of Flanders, built a castle as protection from Viking raids, and gradually a town grew up. Trade came via the nearby village of Damme and its waterway, the Zwin.

As in other Flemish cities, textiles were Bruges' ticket to prosperity. Much trade was connected to England's wool industry, the source of the finest grade of wool, and by the late 13th century Bruges was a major cloth-trading centre. When Philip the Fair, King of France, visited Bruges in

1301, his wife, Joanna of Navarre, was so surprised by the inhabitants' wealth and luxurious clothes that she purportedly claimed: 'I thought I alone was queen, but I see that I have 600 rivals here'.

But the city's increased wealth brought political tension and, after guildsmen refused to pay a new round of taxes in 1302, the army was sent in to garrison the town. Pieter De Coninck, Dean of the Guild of Weavers, and Jan Breydel, Dean of the Guild of Butchers, led a revolt against the 2000-strong army that would go down in Flanders' history books as the Brugse Metten (Bruges Matins). Early in the morning on 18 May, the guildsmen crept into town and murdered anyone who could not correctly pronounce the Flemish phrase *'schild en vriend'* (shield and friend). This revolt sparked a widespread rebellion and led to the Flemish victory against the French six weeks later at the Battle of the Golden Spurs near Kortrijk. Independence was short-lived, though, and the French soon regained control.

In the 14th century Bruges became a key member of the Hanseatic League of Seventeen Cities, a powerful association of northern European trading cities, and the city reached its economic peak. Italian cities such as Genoa, Florence and Venice built trade houses here, and ships laden with exotic goods from all over Europe and further afield docked at the Minnewater, a small lake to the city's south.

Prosperity continued under the dukes of Burgundy, especially Philip the Good (r 1419–67), who arrived in 1430 to marry Isabella of Portugal. Bruges grew fat and by 1500 the population had ballooned to 200, 000, doubling that of London.

Flemish art blossomed and the city's artists known as the Flemish Primitives perfected paintings that are still vivid today.

During the 15th century the Zwin, the waterway linking Bruges to the sea, silted up. Despite attempts to build another canal, the city's economic lifeline was gone. When the headquarters of the Hanseatic League moved from Bruges to Antwerp at the end of the 15th century, many merchants followed, leaving abandoned houses, deserted streets and empty canals. Bruges, a former hub of Europe, slept for 400 years.

The city slowly emerged from its slumber in the early 19th century as tourists passed through en route to the Waterloo battlefield near Brussels. In 1892 Belgian writer and poet Georges Rodenbach published *Bruges-la-Morte* (Bruges the Dead), a novel that beguilingly described the town's forlorn air and alerted the well-heeled to its preserved charm. Curious, wealthy visitors brought much-needed money into Bruges, and sealed its fate as a town frozen in time.

In 1907 the Boudewijnkanaal, a canal linking Bruges to the new port of Zeebrugge, was constructed. Although Zeebrugge suffered extensive damage during both world wars, Bruges escaped unscathed. As the capital of West-Vlaanderen province, it now lives largely off tourism, although it also has a manufacturing centre outside the city that produces glass, electrical goods and chemicals.

Bruges' stint as European City of Culture in 2002 proved that it's more than just a medieval showpiece. A daring red concert hall, the Concertgebouw, was built to celebrate the event, and contemporary came to the historic centre in the form of the Toyo Ito pavilion.

Historic Centre of Brugge

Brugge is an outstanding example of a medieval historic settlement, which has maintained its historic fabric as this has evolved over the centuries, and where original Gothic constructions form part of the town's identity. As one of the commercial and cultural capitals of Europe, Brugge developed cultural links to different parts of the world. It is closely associated with the school of Flemish Primitive painting.

Outstanding Universal Value

The Historic Centre of Brugge is an outstanding example of an architectural ensemble, illustrating significant stages in the commercial and cultural fields in medieval Europe.

Brugge in medieval times was known as a commercial metropolis in the heart of Europe.

The city reflects a considerable exchange of influences on the development of art and architecture, particularly in brick Gothic, which is characteristic of northern Europe and the Baltic. This architecture strongly determines the character of the historic centre of the city.

The 1th century city walls marked the boundaries of the medieval city. Although the walls themselves are lost today, they remain clearly visible, emphasized by the four surviving gates, the ramparts and one of the defence water towers. The medieval street pattern, with main roads leading towards the important public squares, has mostly been preserved, as well as the network of canals which, once used for mercantile traffic, played an important role in the development of the city.

In the 15th century, Brugge was the cradle of the Flemish Primitives and a centre of patronage and painting development for artists such as Jan van Eyck and Hans Memling. Many of their works were exported and influenced painting styles all over Europe. Exceptionally important collections have remained in the city until today.

Even after its economic and artistic peak at the end of the Middle Ages, building and urban development continued, although Brugge mostly missed the 19th-century industrial revolution. In the 18th and 19th centuries, many medieval parcels were joined to larger entities and new quarters were also developed. The most striking examples of large scale post-medieval interventions in the historic centre are the urbanization around Coupure (1751-1755), the Zand and the first railway station (1838), the Theatre quarter (1867), the Koningin Elisabethlaan and Gulden Vlieslaan (1897) and the creation of the Guido Gezelle-neighbourhood (1920-1930).

In the second half of the 20th century, some major changes occurred with Zilverpand (1976), the new Public Library (1975-1978), the new Palace of Justice and Kartuizerswijk (1980), Clarendam (1990) and Colettijnenhof (1997).

Brugge is characterized by a continuity reflected in the relative harmony of changes. As part of this continuity, the late 19th century renovation of facades introduced a Neo-Gothic style that is particular for Brugge. The Brugge 'neo' style of construction and its restoration philosophy became a subject of interest, study and inspiration.

Still an active, living city today, Brugge has preserved the architectural and urban structures which document the different phases of its development including the central Market Place with its belfry, the *Béguinage*, as well as the hospitals, the religious and commercial complexes and the historic urban fabric.

Criterion (ii): The Historic Centre of Brugge bears testimony to a considerable exchange of influences on the development of architecture, and particularly brick Gothic architecture, over a long period of time. As the birthplace of the school of the Flemish Primitives, it has favoured innovative artistic influences in the development of medieval painting.

Criterion (iv): The Historic Centre of Brugge is an outstanding example of an architectural ensemble. The city's public, social and religious institutions illustrate significant stages in the history of commerce and culture in medieval Europe

Criterion (vi): The Historic Centre of Brugge was birthplace of the Flemish Primitives and a centre of patronage and development of painting in the Middle Ages with artists such as Jan van Eyck and Hans Memling.

Authenticity

The Historic Centre of Brugge illustrates continuity on an urban site that has been occupied since the early Middle Ages. Historical records of the town administration and regulations are condensed in the city records from the 13th century onwards.

An area of continuous settlement, the Historic Centre of Brugge has retained the original pattern of streets and places, canals, and open spaces. A very specific skyline of towers and taller civic buildings (such as the cathedral, the belfry and the churches) dominates the city. For the most part, buildings have retained the original parcels of land. The transformations that have taken place over time respect the functional changes in the town, and have become part of its historic authenticity, in a parallel way to other historic cities such as Siena in Italy.

The history of the town is well represented in the urban and architectural structures that harmoniously unify all periods of history since the origin of the city.

Since the second half of the 19th century, much attention has been paid to the history and the architecture of the town, and major debates about modalities followed the international trends in the field of restoration and conservation. This chronological and historical stratification is clearly recognizable in the urban morphology and architecture and is part of the present character of Brugge.

Some modern transformations have occurred in the property, but their impact on the whole property is considered minor.

Integrity

The overall urban structure still represents the medieval "egg-shaped" model that can be seen on the map of Marcus Gerards (1562). Apart from the religious wars in the 16th century and the French Revolution, Brugge more or less escaped the devastation associated with other conflicts that marked this part of Europe, including the First and Second World Wars. Similarly, the 19thcentury industrial revolution had almost no impact on the basic structure of the historic town, with the exception of the railway station in the southwest of the city.

The property includes all urban structures, associated ensembles and individual buildings that reflect its commercial and artistic development and the legacy of 19th century restoration philosophies.

The remarkable visual coherence that characterises its urban form is vulnerable to rebuilding. Large-scale development in proximity to the property could adversely impact the relationship between the property and its setting.

Protection and management requirements

Since 1972, the municipal Department for Conservation and Heritage Management guides evaluates and closely monitors all changes in the urban environment, in collaboration with the regional heritage services. The specific municipal building regulations are very strict and include a *non modificandi* agreement when city funding is provided to carry out restoration works.

Around half of all buildings within the historic centre are either listed or registered in the Flemish inventory of Built Heritage and in the city's Heritage Evaluation Map (a dynamic instrument), which serves as a policy and management tool. In the case of listed buildings and sites, there is a mandatory and binding advice from the regional heritage authorities.

The coordination, communication and promotion of the World Heritage property is taken up as before by the municipal Department for Conservation and Heritage Management, in close collaboration with all partners on municipal and regional level.

Conservation and restoration of monuments and sites is based on a restoration philosophy and tradition in which the original materials and construction technique are the starting point. New constructions in the inner city never occur without a thorough art-historical evaluation and always respect the historical authenticity. As a rule, new constructions respect parcelling, pattern, heights, materials etc. of the surroundings. Large-scale developments in proximity of the property remain a possible threat and therefore require particular attention.

As a result, a World Heritage Management Plan was made in 2012, coordinated by the city of Brugge and its Department for Conservation and Heritage Management, which is a team of specialists qualified in the history of art, the history of Bruges in general and restoration philosophy and practice. This Management Plan aims to foster appropriate development within agreed constraints in relation to the acknowledged characteristics of defined areas. A UNESCO Expert Commission was set up by the city council in 2011, supported the development of a Management Plan in 2012 and continues to provide advice.

In continuation of the Management Plan, Conservation Plans are being prepared, as well as Preservation Plans, Detailed Survey Plans and a Thematic Spatial Implementation Plan for the historic urban landscape, covering the whole World Heritage property.

Historically and typologically, the city is home to a mixture of functions. This diversity is an essential urban feature that needs to be preserved and protected. This element, along with the historical urban structure and the specific and diverse architectural characteristics that reflect the evolution of Brugge, are at the essence of the future management of the property. However, Brugge is a living city, in which developments and changes should be possible but only in appropriate locations and with respect for the urban morphology of closed urban plots limited by streets and laneways in the historic centre.

Expansion is possible in the greater Brugge region, which historically and politically was linked with the city ("Brugs Ommeland", or the surroundings of Brugge) and Zeebrugge (the seaport of Brugge). In order to protect the setting of the property, effective links between the interests of this wider city of Brugge and the property, in terms of planning and protection, are needed and in progress. Important views from and to the property need to be protected and will be incorporated in the urban planning tools.

From a touristic point of view, Brugge has made considerable efforts to manage the impact of visitors. The development of durable cultural tourism of high quality will continue to remain the basis of the municipal policy in this regard, with a specific attention to events and activities related to the Flemish Primitives.

Travel and Tourism

Good wine doesn't need a crown. There is no place in Belgim where so many remains of Middle Ages can be found as in Bruges. The history of Damme has always been closely related to the history of Bruges. Together they knew their times of glory, which made them infamous all over the known world. But they also went down together when the Zwin silted up and seaships could no longer reach Bruges or one of her ports.

Bruges said to have originated from a Gallo-Roman settlement some 2000 years ago. At that time trade via the sea already took place here.

On what is now know as the "Burg", there used to be a stronghold in the middle of the 9th century. The port was accessible directly from the sea until the middle of the 11th century. At that moment in time, the town already had grown to an international commercial center.

Slowly however the connection to the sea silted up. A stormflood in 1134 created a new bay, the Zwin, which reached till Damme. Damme became the port of Bruges, lateron Sluis and Bruges continued to be prosperous. Unfortunately, the Zwin silted up too and seaships could no longer reach Damme. Throughout the entire history of the town, the citizens of Bruges continuously tried to maintain their connection to the sea. A last attempt to reach the Westerschelde via a canal (the present Damse Vaart) was undertaken by Napoleon. Because of his loss in the war, the canal never was finished and stops in Sluis. Nowadays the town has again a great seaport, namely Zeebruges.

Throughout the Middle Ages, the region around Bruges was one of the most prosperous of Europe and because of that a very wanted area for foreign rulers. The county of Flanders came to existence here and Bruges was its capital. At the peak of its power and wealth, Flanders was a lot larger than what it is now. Although the one foreign power after the other ruled the region, the Flemish cities succeeded in keeping a great level of indepence for a long time.

One of the most significant events was the rising of the Flemish against the French occupier in 1302. At this event, French troops, garrisoned in the castle of Male, were put out of action. One night, the French army (Leliaerts) that occupied the town itself was slaughtered by the Flemish (Klauwaerts). Till that night, the Flemish had been hiding in Damme. This were what is called the "Brugse Metten". In the battle that followed these events (Battle of the Golden Spurs, Courtray 11 July 1302) the French king's army of knights was defeated by the Flemish. In the battles that followed, the Flemish cities were not always so successful.

In 1384, the Flanders were gouverned by Burgundy. This was the result of the marriage of Margareta of Male (daughter of Lodewijk of Male, 24th count of Flanders) and Philips, duke of Burgundy. The new rulers also tried to submit the town, in order to collect as much taxes as possible. The dukes had gread need of money to finance their costly wars against France. The citizens of Bruges however, were very attached to their independence and privileges and regularly this lead to uprisings. In 1482, duke Maximilian of Austria (who had just become widower of Maria of Burgundy) was captured when he tried to break tho town's power and wanted to impose more taxes. His collaborators were tortured on Bruges' Marketsquare and condemned to the death. The most known story is the one of Pieter Lanckhals, who was decaputated, after which his head was placed on a pike above the Gentpoort. The days when Burgundy ruled the town however, was a time of great prosperity. Their departure was the beginning of the end.

After Burgundy came Spain, that brought the Southern Netherlands under their government. It was then that Damme became a bastion. Then cam the French revolution and Napoleon. In that period, the town was plundered in administrative way.

The industrial revolution passed by the town and by the middle of the 19th century, Bruges had become the poorest town in Flanders. After that period, tourism began and nowadays millions of tourists visit the town because of its rich cultural heritage and its monuments. This town is a true open-air museum; lots of buildings that date back to the glory days are still intact. That's what makes Bruges one of a kind.

The wealth of Bruges is due to many factors. There was the trade with entire Europe (from Scandinavia and England to the cities in de Mediteranean Sea). The region had a very flourishing cloth industry and lateron also the famous lace of Bruges became a very popular export product. The arrival of foreign Hanzes and representatives from other cities and countries, transformed the town to an important financial center, you could say a Wallstreet avant-la-lettre. Prosperity also brought art in the town. Think about the priceless Flemish Primitives. But also a lot of other artefacts are sign of the rich cultural life. Bruges has lots of museums where you can 'taste' of all this.

The decay of the region is due to a combination of various factors. Not only the wars with foreign rulers, but also internal fights with other towns made the area less attractive (and lucrative). The silting up of the Zwin estuary made trade over sea more and more difficult. Epidemics like the plague made a lot of casualties, Geuzen (protestant religious fighters) plundered the town and traders more and more left as a consequence. The industrial revolution in England finally meant the end of the blooming textile industry in Flanders...

Guide to Brugge

Sightseeing in Brugge what to see. Complete travel guide

Bruges is located in the Belgium province of West-Flanders that is approximately 2 hours away from Utrecht (Holland). In the 9th century this town was conquered by the Vikings, that's why the name of the city is likely to come from the Scandinavian word 'bryggia' that means 'port'. Bruges is situated not far from the North Sea, so it has become quite an important international trade centre. Later, in the Middle Ages, a big wall was built around Bruges.

Beguinage. This is one of the main places of interest in Bruges. It was founded in the 13th century, though the majority of white houses appeared only in the 17th and 18th centuries. The arch bridge, which forms the entrance to the palace, was built in 1570. Beguine sisterhood doesn't live there anymore, and this place now belongs to the Benedictines from De Wijngaard convent. The house under the first number serves as a museum, so everyone can get an idea of Beguine's way of life. The kitchen, the dining-room and bedrooms are furnished in the style of the 17th century. Initially, the main chapel was made of wood, but, unfortunately, it burnt down. In 1605 a new chapel in the baroque style was built on its site. Fortunately, it has remained undamaged till our times. Nowadays, everyone is welcome to visit the chapel. The chapel is famous for the oldest image of Our Lady in Bruges. The image was created in 1240. There is also an altar with the alabaster sculpture of Christ of the 17th century on the right.

Beguinage is situated near Minnewater Lake, which used to be a part of the canal that connected Bruges and Ghent. Nowadays it's just a small picturesque lake with beautiful swans swimming in it. There is an interesting legend in Bruges, which is connected with swans. When Maximilian of Austria raised the taxes again, Bruges citizens rebelled and captivated the city. They also beheaded the former town head, whose name was Pieter Lanchals (it means 'long neck'). When Maximilian got the power back, he made an order, according to which swans (because they also have long necks) are to be bred till the end of the world in Bruges. Do you know how to differ a female swan from a male swan? You can guess by the mark - male swans have it on the right clutch and female swans have it on the left one.

The chapel of the Holy Blood. The chapel of the Holy Blood was built on the site of Basilius Chapel of the 12th century. The beautiful church is a wonderful example of the Romanesque style. Visitors will see a colored wooden image of the

Virgin with the baby (approximately 1300) on the right nave. Initially, the chapel of the Holy Blood was built in the Romanesque style, but in the 15th century after the reconstruction it turned into a Gothic chapel. During the French revolution the basilica was ruined, and then it was rebuilt from the very beginning. Entering the church is free, but you will have to pay in order to visit the Museum of the Holy Blood. As the legend says, in 1150 a part of linen with blood of Jesus was brought from Jerusalem. The duke that had brought it ordered to build Basilius Chapel, where the relic was to be kept. We can't say for sure whether it's truth of not. Scientists have a theory that most likely the legend tells about Duke Baldwin IX, who brought it from the crusade to Constantinople in 1203.

The blood of Jesus is kept in an incredibly beautiful casket of 1817. Jan Crabbe, the master who created the casket, used approximately 30 kg of gold and silver, and more than a hundred of jewels. Every year on Ascension Day a solemn ceremony takes place in Bruges. The procession carries the casket through the streets of the city. The museum located nearby is a great place to learn the detailed history of the relic and the basilica. One can also look at the silver crown of the 15th century, which was presented by Maria of Burgundy, and some other interesting paintings.

Grote Market. The central square of the city is located in the very heart of Bruges. At the square you'll find a lot of marvellous historical buildings. The Belfort built in the 12th century is one of them. The tower of this building is 83 meter high and it deflects to the left for a meter. Grote Market is also home to various cafes and restaurants. By the way, carriage excursions also start there. This is a very popular kind of entertainment in Bruges.

Halve Maan. Halve Maan is a brewery, where the sort of beer called Brugse Zot (you can taste it in Bruges only) is produced. Long time ago the brewery also produced another sort of beer - Straffe Hendrik. However, nowadays this beer is not produced anymore. Since 1564 this brewery has been located in the same building at Walplein Square, in the historical center of Bruges. Nowadays, the excursions to the brewery have become very popular. Of course, beer degustation is the culmination of every excursion.

The City Hall. The fabulous City Hall was built by order of Jan Rugirs. It was finished in 1421. The front side of the building is beautifully decorated with small towers. Wall paintings are especially interesting. The City Hall is situated at de Burg Square.

Family trip with kids

Family trip to Brugge with children. Ideas on where to go with your child

Simply no family vacation in Bruges can happen without visiting confectioneries and cafes, walking in picturesque parks and attending interesting museums. This wonderful city will certainly please sweet tooth travelers, who will be able to enjoy magnificent Belgian chocolate and various chocolate desserts simply everywhere. Do you want to pamper your kids with some premium sweets? If so, head to DUMON Chocolatier as this confectionery is considered one of the best in the city. Here visitors are welcome to choose from hundreds of types of chocolates, cakes, and cookies.

Moreover, visitors can order chocolates or a cake in accordance with individual design and preferences.

A visit to the Chocolate Museum (Choco Story) will be a wonderful continuation of your exploration of delicious Belgian chocolate. The museum is located in one of the most beautiful historic buildings of the city. Visitors to the museum will learn how cocoa beans are grown and how chocolate is cooked. Choco Story exhibits an interesting collection of items, all of which, as it's not hard to guess, are made of chocolate. Moreover, the museum regularly hosts various interesting master classes for children, during which kids will learn to cook sweets by themselves.

Travellers, who prefer more active pastime, may prefer a visit to Boudewijn Seapark. This amusement park is located in the southern part of Bruges. Inside, visitors will find various water slides, a beautiful swimming pool, and special playgrounds for children. The park is proud of its dolphinarium, so spectacular shows with dolphins and seals as main performers take place nearly every day at the park.

If you're tired of walking and want to diversify your vacation with calmer activities, it's time to make a boat ride on Bruges canals. Children will be particularly fond of boat excursions as they will be able not only to make a refreshing and entertaining ride, but also feed birds that live there ducks and swans.

There are many toy shops and other stores that will be liked by children in Bruges. Kathe Wohlfahrt, which sells Christmas ornaments, is one of the most unusual shops in the city. It works all year round. Christmas celebrations are the most liked time of the year in Bruges, so the choice of decorations is truly amazing. Here visitors can buy exclusive ornaments and toys made of wood and glass. Everything at the shop is handmade, so every decoration is unique.

Nearly all children adore potato fries, and in Bruges they have an amazing opportunity to visit a museum dedicated to their favorite food. Frietmuseum offers a rich collection of items with interesting historic artifacts. Guests of the museum will learn that for the first time potatoes were brought to Europe from Peru and will see interesting devices that were used to peel and slice potatoes hundreds of years ago. There is a charming café on the ground floor of the building, which signature dish is not hard to guess.

When it's hot outside, there is nothing better than relaxing in serene atmosphere, making a bicycle ride with kids on shadowy valleys and then having a picnic in a picturesque place. All these and more you will find in Astrid Park. It is located in the heart of the city not far from popular tourist routes, but at the same time this park is distinguished by calm and peaceful atmosphere. It is possible to spend hours walking on picturesque roads, admiring the look of giant trees or feeding swans. There are wonderful athletic fields and playgrounds for children in the park.

Cuisine & restaurants

Cuisine of Brugge for gourmets. Places for dinner best restaurants

You can find cozy pubs and restaurants almost on every street of the city. Speaking of pricing policy in the gastronomic facilities of this place, it is worth noting that all most prestigious and expensive restaurants are located near Burg and Markt Squares. Tourists and students traditionally choose local kiosks called "fricatens", where you can buy everyone's favorite French fried potato and other snacks. The majority of the prestigious restaurants open after 6 pm. Among the fashionable restaurants of the city we surely should mention De Drie Zintuigen, which serves gourmet delicacies and rarest wines. Bruges is a true paradise for fans of drinking, because simply every bar and pub in Bruges features dozens of types of Belgian beer.

Thus, De Garre pub offers visitors to choose from as much as one hundred types of beer. It has its own brewery, which produces an exclusive brand of beer called Triple de Garre. Brugs Beertje pub is famous for its everlasting funny and relaxed atmosphere. In addition to beer you will always find here excellent meals. Perhaps, Vlissinghe tavern is the oldest institution of this kind in Bruges. It was opened in 1515. Here guests will be offered to try national cuisine in its classic version. Of course, there are more exotic facilities in Bruges. Narai Thai restaurant is one of them. Thai delicacies form the basis of its menu and, the restaurant's chef never ceases to amaze visitors with original author's masterpieces and a masterful combination of oriental spices.

Huidevettershuis restaurant is located right in the center of the city. The specialties of this place are traditional Flemish soup, roasted rabbit and home-made ham. In addition to widest choice meat delicacies, visitors are welcome to try vegetarian dishes, as well as excellent pickled herring. The opening of De Karmeliet restaurant was held in 1996. Since that time it has been considered one of the best restaurants devoted to the Flemish cuisine in the city. Here you can order fine fish soup with shrimps and numerous vegetable salads, and, of course, best Belgian cheese. In addition to the national cuisine, the restaurant serves interesting Bhavani Indian delicacies, resisting which is simply impossible despite the fact whether you are a gourmet, or a usual visitor. The restaurant features a separate children's menu, so it is the ideal choice for families.

Besides traditional Belgian beer, waffles, and chocolate, Bruge can offer a range of interesting national delicacies to guests of the city. Tourists on a budget usually like to order French fries that are considered the most popular "street food" in Bruges. Local people started cooking French fries yet in the 16th century. Nowadays, crispy roasted potatoes are available in all local cafes and restaurants specializing in the national cuisine. French fries are served as a garnish to many popular dishes, including mussels that are incredibly popular in Belgium. There are even local cafes that specialize exclusively in cooking French fries.

Beer fans in Bruges will be genuinely delighted with a visit to De Halve Maan. This old brewery has been operating since 1546. It organizes interesting excursions for tourists, during which visitors can find out about secrets of brewing different sorts of beer. Connoisseurs of the foamy drink are recommended to try local Kvak beer during their stay in Bruges. This beer has not only unusual taste but also a very original serving the beer is served in glasses of a particular shape.

National cuisine restaurants in Bruges offer their guests to try a range of traditional dishes with the game. Many of these dishes have been cooked in accordance with unchanged recipes for several centuries. For example, the Huidevettershuis restaurant has several signature dishes, including rabbit roasted in a peculiar way. Local restaurants specializing in the national cuisine also offer delicious, mouthwatering steaks. Menus of the traditional restaurants will pleasantly surprise travelers keen on seafood. They are recommended to try mussels cooked in dozens of ways and the famous fish soup with prawns.

Rabbit stew is a famous gastronomic specialty of Bruges. Locals also like eel stew. Various dishes with chicken meat are also very widespread in the city. It is important to mention that chicken is less popular in other regions of Belgium. Fans of desserts should not forget to visit the Museum of Chocolate in Bruges that is not only one of the biggest venues of its kind in the country but also in the world. The museum's visitors will learn a lot of interesting information about the peculiarities of different kinds of Belgian chocolate and, of course, sample the ever popular dessert. Once the excursion is over, visitors are welcome to purchase fabulous chocolate gifts for their friends and family.

Traditions & lifestyle

Colors of Brugge traditions, festivals, mentality and lifestyle

The residents of the city celebrate their main national holiday on July 21. On this day in 1831 the great King Leopold became the ruler of the kingdom, declaring its independence. Since that time July 21 has become a significant event and the time of conducting various folk festivals, which are traditionally accompanied by lively street performances, festivals and fairs.

Accuracy and diligence have remained one of the main traits of local residents. Starting from ancient times, this place has become widely famous for high quality lace and weapons. It's amazing and surprising that the masters of those time could equally control both thin and fragile materials, and steel. Currently Bruges is a major center for production of electronics, so the local people never cease to amaze visitors with their talents.

Travelers can buy beautiful jewelry as a souvenir in Bruges. It is believed that the local jewelers cut diamonds according to special rules and use the same method of processing gemstones as their ancestors many centuries ago. The local inhabitants are very friendly to tourists who are just captivated by the kindness and hospitality of the city's people.

An important religious holiday called Day of the Holy Blood is celebrated annually in Bruges. The celebration does not have the exact date and depends on what day Easter is celebrated this year. It is believed that local residents started celebrating the Feast of the Holy Blood in 1149 when the Flemish Count brought a valuable relic to the city - a vessel with the blood of Jesus Christ. The count won this valuable relic in a crusade. When residents found out about this relic, they turned to the count with a request to bow to the religious shrine. Gradually, the rumors about the precious vessel spread throughout the country and further, attracting pilgrims from different countries to Bruges. Currently over one hundred thousands of pilgrims come to the city on this memorable day. A massive procession is held in the city, the participants of which are dressed in ancient costumes of the clergy and knights.

The city of Bruges is the place where the counterpoint is seen at every step. An amazing combination of the astonishing medieval architecture of Western Europe and modern culture create the unforgettable atmosphere. By the way, did you know that Bruges is also called the "Northern Venice"? The number of channels and waterways flowing into the North Sea can spot Venice itself. Also, people of Bruges enjoy celebrating various holidays and welcome tourists from all over the world. The biggest attention they pay to religious holidays, and one of the most honoured is the Procession of the Holy Blood. It is the considerable religious event making a part of cultural heritage of the country.

Annually, tens of thousands of people take part in a solemn procession, putting on suits of ancient knights and monks. This procession represents and reminds about the first crusades when the Flemish count received a sacred the relic of Blood of Christ.

Feest in 't Park, is one of the main events of summer. Every year, at the end of June, in the Bruges central park hundreds of families gather to enjoy time during the event. Tourists are always welcomed to share the joy and fun. During the festival you will be offered to enjoy various entertainments for free, starting from master classes in crafts and finishing with tasting the beer. In the centre of the park you here is a big open-air stage, where musicians from different countries will entertain you. Moreover, you can get a free lesson of folk dances of Belgian, African, Indian and Arab cultures. Within the festival, you have a chance to purchase various crafts and souvenirs on the trade fair. In a gastronomic zone, visitors will be suggested to try national dishes and to buy unusual products.

In the case, you missed Feest in 't Park in June, you will have the chance to have fun during another festival called Moods! It takes place at the end of July and in the first days of August. Within two full weeks, a lot of musical performances and unforgettable fireworks will be established in the most notable places of interest in Bruges like the yard of Beffroi belltower. In a unique environment, you will be able to enjoy the best national and international performances at one of eight evening concerts. Moreover, concerts will take place at Burg Square and the entrance is free.

Culture: sights to visit

Culture of Brugge. Places to visit old town, temples, theaters, museums and palaces

Thanks to quivering and respect of citizens, Bruges is home to numerous architectural and historical monuments. The old castle of Counts of Flanders is located not far away from Bourg. The castle was built in the 9th century. A walk through the beautiful square will help to

There are also natural attractions in Bruges. Minnewater Lake is one of them. It is considered the most romantic place in the city, and so many interesting superstitions and legends are connected with it. On evenings you can see many romantic couples on the lake who come here to admire the sunset and enjoy the intimate atmosphere. Among the major attractions of the city is also the bell tower of Church of Notre-Dame, which height estimates 122 meters. The bell tower is made in the Gothic style. This is also the second tallest building of the country.

Christ the Savior Cathedral is another bright religious landmark. It was founded in the middle of the 7th century. It is natural that nothing has remained from the original building. During the centuries of its history the church has survived in four fires, and has suffered greatly during the French Revolution. The cathedral, which travelers can see today, was built in the end of the 15th century. Talking about religious things, we simple can't fail to ignore and the Jerusalem church. The building of the church was completed in 1470. Experts in ancient architecture often compare it with its famous Church of the Holy Sepulcher. Fine stained glass windows are the main decoration of the cathedral. They were made in the early 15th century. The hall of the church is also the tomb of its founder - Anselm Adorno. This church is one of the few religious monuments, which has never been subjected to strong restructuring during its centuries-long history.

Art lovers should not forget to visit Groeninge museum, which exhibits a rich collection of paintings. Among the cultural institutions of the city there are also some highly original ones, such as Museum of French Fried Potato, Chocolate Museum and Museum of Diamonds.

Torture Museum Oude Steen is an equally remarkable place where you can look at how inventive people can be here is a huge collection of torture materials. The faint-hearted and children are better off not going to this institution, but they are welcome to visit all other places. The Bruges Beer Experience is sure to capture everyone's interest, where, in addition to learning everything about the history of beer, you can taste a drink and choose the best variety for yourself, as a bonus. Among other museums we would note Sint-Janshospitaal, which is one of the first hospitals in the whole of Europe. In addition, the hospital is a wonderful example of medieval architecture.

It is difficult to imagine a more wonderful and enchanting place in Bruges than Ezelpoort. It seems like not just any gate, but a gate to a real paradise for lovers of history for sure. The attraction encompasses a lake which is home to swans of heavenly beauty, considered to be a kind of "paradise for animals" in Eden. Beguinage is another place where the tender soul of history aficinados will find true pleasure. However, everyone shoud go for a walk here as this is yet another peaceful place with swans swimming in the lake. Also, those wishing to experience an incomparable pacification are advised to visit Sint-Janshuismolen.

You can go for a nice walk on The Markt, a chic area where at every step you will meet an interesting building. You can also visit the Huidenvettersplein, where in addition to the cultural experience you will be visiting local restaurants and cafes, each of which is remarkable for its matchless interesting interior. In other words, it is in fact a continuation of cultural enrichment. Near the Market Square you can find the Provinciaal Hof one of the symbols of Bruges, the gem of Gothic architecture.

There are two buildings in the city; simply put, failure to visit them would almost be considered sacrilegious, if not downright cruel. Firstly, is the bell tower Belfort, rising to the top of which you can see the incredibly beautiful city of Bruges open up. If you visit this place in the evening, then there will be no limit to the pleasure you will get. The second place is the Tower of Poertoren, an excellent example of the Romanesque style of architecture. Film lovers will recognize the footage from the film "In Bruges" although there are plenty of such places that could be recognized thanks to the film.

Fans of mysterious and mystical things will be delighted by visiting two places in the city: first, the Site Oud Sint-Jan (located next to Sint-Janshospitaal), where you can look at the tools of medieval medicine, imbued with the atmosphere of that period. Visitors are demonstrated dreadful scenes of the then conducted surgery. In addition, there is a collection of Hans Memling's paintings, which brings conflicting feelings. Another place Rozenhoedkaai is the embankment, on which you can make an unforgettable romantic walk. Something mystical emits from this place.

Attractions & nightlife

City break in Brugge. Active leisure ideas for Brugge attractions, recreation and nightlife Boating on the canals of the city remains one of the most favorite pastimes for both visitors and locals. During such ride you will be able not only enjoy the beautiful scenery, but also learn about the history of the city. Cycling is a no less attractive option for wonderful pastime. You will find large number of bike rental offices in Bruges. As a rule, they are located near popular hotels of the city. Fans of more unusual entertainments are advised to make a ride around the city on a horse-drawn carriage. A walk along stone streets and elegant squares will be a real journey into the past.

Bruges will be surely liked by nightlife lovers and people who enjoy entertainments. B-in is considered one of the most popular nightclubs of the city. It is located on Mariastraat Street. A cozy bar with the same name is located next to the night club. It offers to visitors a huge selection of exotic cocktails, beer and branded snacks. The Cactus club will definitely attract lovers of various musical styles. On evenings, numerous dancing enthusiasts move their feet to the club. Several times a week experienced dancers organize here different classes for beginners. Finally, if you are tired of loud music and want some rest, a cozy bar is at your service.

During your walk in the shops make sure you don't forget to buy traditional souvenirs - fine lace and chocolate. Steenstraat, Mariastraat and Simon Stevinplein are best places for shopping. Here visitors will find widest choice of boutiques and shopping pavilions. "Rococo" is considered the best lace store of the city, so no female will be able to leave this place without buying a memorable gift. «The Chocolate Line» is the best place to go if your aim is best chocolate. At a glance it may resemble a boutique or a jewelry shop - sweets are laid out on beautiful display cases with lighting. The air in «The Chocolate Line» is soaked in the enchanting aroma of chocolate, which captivates from the first minute. Another popular "souvenir" that travelers love to buy is, without a doubt, cheese. In a shopping pavilion named «Diksmuids Boterhuis» you will find more than three hundred varieties of cheese that is produced in local factories. There is also a real gourmet cheese, imported from Switzerland, France and England.

In a tiny city of Bruges, there are many interesting ways to spend time with pleasure. If you consider yourself an active traveller, then the variety of entertainments will brighten your day and leave joyful emotions. For example, amazing opportunity to explore the city and see it from with a bird's eye view is to make the most real tourist feat to rise on top of a watchtower. Here you will be astonished by the look at the city from the height of 107 meters. Those who are not scared of height and really have the desire to visit this amazing observation deck should take into consideration that you will need to walk upstairs which contains 366 abrupt steps. The award for this heavy walk is worth it a smart view of the city.

If you would rather have a smooth walk along the streets than abrupt rise up then you must discover the narrowest street in whole Bruges.

This street has the strangest name you have ever heard - Blinde Ezelstraat, in English it means The Street of Blind Donkey. Just because of its name you must check it! The best time to see it is during morning hours. The reason is simple, during the morning the street is empty and you can make a lot of great photos. The most exciting and unforgettable way to discover the small city of Bruges is to take the flight on the balloon. Bruges Ballooning service provides these astonishing adventures that will not leave you with a bunch of emotions. The price of the tour is about 180 euros. You can choose and book the tour independently by visiting the official website or join some tourist companies.

If you are a great fan of an active recreation than you should pay attention to Boudewijn Seapark amusement park. It is located in several kilometres from Bruges and is the only park in the country which includes a dolphinarium. Boudewijn Seapark works from April to October, the dolphinarium works all the year round. It is possible to visit it even in the winter. The visiting hours are the following: from 10 till 18-00. The cost of tickets varies from 9 to 23 euros, depending on the age of the visitor. The most notable attraction you can find in the park is the Springride. This attraction allows children, whose height is above one meter. Here you will be able to feel a free fall from the height of seven meters. For children, the so-called Bobo attraction will be especially interesting. In fact, it is more than ten attractions under the same roof placed on the area of 2500 square meters.

Tips for tourists

Preparing your trip to Brugge: advices & hints things to do and to obey

1. Weather in Bruges is quite changeable and cold. Even in summer the temperature rarely rises above +21°C. Tourists are recommended to take some warm clothes with them and make long walks only with an umbrella, because rain can start here really suddenly.

2. Those, who plan to travel around the city, can buy a special ticket. It can be valid for one day only or a certain number of trips.

3. Guests are not recommended to rent a car to travel using it on narrow streets of the city as it will be very problematic. The city has only several major car parks which are located in the central area. Bicycle will become the best alternative to a car here.

4. Travelers, who plan to attend various tours and museums, should consider purchasing Brugge City Card. It provides discounts on visiting main museums the city, its public transportation, and bicycle rental. It will help you to save up to 200 euros. The card can be purchased for 48 or 72 hours. Moreover, travelers under 26 years will get a discount for this purchase.

5. Tips are included in the bills of almost all restaurants and cafes, so leaving additional money for waiter is not necessary.

6. It is not recommended to discuss such themes vibrant historical events, local culture and history with the locals. Many of them are very sensitive and may be offended because of a careless phrase. The royal family is another taboo subject for conversation.

7. Despite the fact that many customs and traditions of the local people may recall you the traditions of the French, you should never compare their culture with other countries.

8. The locals are very friendly to tourists who try to speak their native language, but are very offended when visitors try to copy their accent.

Shopping in Brugge

Shopping in Brugge authentic goods, best outlets, malls and boutiques

A leisurely stroll along Walplein street is the best way to start shopping spree in Bruges. It is a very beautiful historic street, which has preserved many spectacular buildings in national style. Nowadays, interesting shops are located in these picturesque houses. You can buy handmade crafts, fresh local food, and wonderful beer from local breweries. On this street there are several colourful national restaurants. In summer they equip spacious lovely terraces at the door.

Flea Market located by the canal is a real city's sight. Many tourists come here in search of original vintage souvenirs. It is here, that you can buy a lot of unique objects of the past. Here they sell beautiful old furniture, paintings and books, old porcelain crafts. You can bind walking around the market with a rest in local restaurants, where visitors are offered traditional fried sausages and delicious beer.

For many, shopping in Bruges is associated with a local chocolate tasting at all times. Those who have a sweet tooth should include a visit to the Chocolate Line confectionery in their program, where they can taste the most popular and original sorts of Belgian chocolate. It sells beautiful figured chocolate. You can taste exotic sorts of chocolate with pepper and spices, as well as classic sorts with nuts and fruit additions. This is a candy store with an open-plan kitchen, so all customers can follow the work of confectioners. Luxurious chocolate is sold by weight. Customers will always have an opportunity to purchase a jar of exclusive chocolate massage cream.

In Bruges, you will find a lot of original souvenir shops selling thematic articles for lovers of beer. De Bier Tempel store remains the best one in this category for many years. It is located next to the Market Square. In this store a huge choice of popular sorts of beer is presented, yet, they sell beer steins, lighters, magnets and other souvenirs with beer symbols. Here, you can find excellent gift bags, and taste the most popular varieties of foam drink.

In the city there is also a specialty store for cheese enthusiasts. It is Diksmuids Boterhuis. In this trading pavilion over a hundred kinds of cheeses are presented, among which you will find unique domestic varieties, and very rare ones, which are more costly. Gourmets will definitely find some good old pampering for themselves. You can taste cheses before purchasing. This store is also mainly focused on tourists, that's why some sorts of cheese are traditionally sold in beautiful gift boxes.

Another interesting symbol of Bruges is lace. Numerous historical lace workshops are located all over the city. Bruges Kantcentrum (the Lace Centre) is a famous city's attraction. It is located in an old 15th-century building. Here, well-known local lacemakers present their works. You can buy incredibly beautiful memorable gifts for yourself and your loved ones. Thematic exhibitions and master classes are often held in this trade pavillion. In Bruges, as in any major tourist city, there is a huge choice of classic clothing stores and shopping centers. But it's not necessary to limit a touristic program by shopping expeditions only for such stores

Unusual weekend

How to spend top weekend in Brugge ideas on extraordinary attractions and sites

Miniature Bruges is famous for its unique historic buildings, but observation of architecture landmarks is not the only possible pastime. Actually, there are many ways for travellers to enjoy a non-standard vacation in the city. There are some interesting places and entertainments that are not well-known to the majority of travellers, so you have a chance to enjoy an unforgettable vacation in Bruges and make your friends jealous afterwards.

Guests of Bruges have an opportunity to make a true act of tourist bravery and go up to the top of the guardian tower and look at the city from a height of 107 meters. Travellers, who want to reach such an amazing observation deck, should be prepared to go up a very steep ladder with as many as 366 steps. However, the reward a breath-taking view of the city is worth the effort.

If steep climbs are not your cup of tea and you prefer unhurried walks instead, it will be fun to find the narrowest street in the city! The street has quite an unusual name - Blinde Ezelstraat or the street of a blind donkey. It is better to come to this area in the morning as closer to noon it's always crowded with tourists and it's getting quite complicated to walk on this street, leave alone making interesting photographs.

One more way to have an exciting morning is to make a boat ride on canals. This romantic activity will be liked not only by romantic couples, but also by people who are fond of historic buildings. It is possible to see some historic and architectural landmarks of Bruges in their full splendor only from the waterside. Morning is the best time for such a boat ride as streets are not yet full of other travellers.

Rides on canals of the city are quite a popular and sought after activity, but not everyone knows that it's possible to explore old streets and landmarks in horse carts. Beautiful carts with well-groomed horses can be seen in many central squares of Bruges, including Grote Markt, and travellers are welcome to rent them. As this is quite an expensive entertainment, experienced travellers recommend making such a ride with three or four other people in order to save.

If during your visit to Belgium you want to attend one of old breweries, head to De Halve maan. This brewery was opened yet in 1546, and it's famous not only for rich history and magnificent beer, but also for interesting excursions that regularly take place there. During such a tour, visitors will learn how the beer is made and sample best sorts of the popular drink. In the end, visitors will be guided to the observation deck on the roof of the ancient brewery in order to admire the charming views of Bruges.

If romantic vacation was the primary purpose of visiting Bruges, don't forget to visit Lake Minnevater also known as the Lake of Love. This is a true piece of serenity and calmness, and it's simple to spend hours relaxing and admiring the surrounding nature. The lake is also famous for a large number of birds that live there. It's even possible to hand feed majestic swans.

Chocolate and beer mugs remain the most popular souvenirs from Bruges. Travellers, who want to bring a more unusual gift, are recommended to visit the teapot shop. This shop is located near the central square on the street that leads to the old town. The unusual shop sells one-of-a-kind teapots that can hardly be seen anywhere else, for example, teapots that look like a car or a toilet bowl. Besides that, you will find rare types of tea and delicious Belgian chocolate there.

Accommodation

Extraordinary hotels

Best choice for your unusual city break in Brugge

Hotel Fevery
From Brugge center - 0.8 km

There are many interesting and peculiar hotels in Bruges. They will be certainly liked by travelers who want to organize a truly unforgettable vacation. Located not far away from the Market Square, Hotel Fevery occupies a beautiful historic building. For many years this hotel has been run by the same family. An important fact Hotel Fevery is an environment conscious hotel. Only natural materials were used during the latest restoration. Guestrooms come with beautiful antique furniture and genuine artworks. The hotel will be liked by travelers who are concerned about their healthy lifestyle every morning they will be treated with fresh fruit and homemade jam.

Hotel Monsieur Ernest
From Brugge center - 0.5 km

Guests of the ancient Belgian city have an opportunity to spend several days in a real aristocratic residence. Such an opportunity is offered by Hotel Monsieur Ernest that occupies a unique building of the 14th century. More than 600 years ago the building belonged to one of the richest dukes in the country. Despite such an honorable age, some elements of the original design can be seen even nowadays, including the wooden ladder with forged banisters, arched passages, carved columns and other stone and wood decorations. This magnificent hotel is a great opportunity to see and feel the atmosphere of the historic past of Bruges.

Hotel Maraboe
From Brugge center - 0.7 km

Hotel Maraboe is a no less interesting place. The beautiful building of the hotel dates back to the 18th century. Originally, a brewery was located there. Nowadays, the unique hotel offers 14 rooms decorated in modern style. The ground floor of the building was turned into a fantastically looking gym with the arched stone ceiling.

Charlie Rockets Youth Hostel
From Brugge center - 0.3 km

The choice of quality hostels and budget hotels is really wide in Bruges. Charlie Rockets Youth Hostel is often called the most unusual and creative hostel in the city. Located just several minutes away from the Market Square, this hostel features truly creative and colorful design. Charlie Rockets Youth Hostel is open in a historic building and some elements of design, such as fragments of the original wooden carcass, remind visitors that they stay at an antique place. The bar has become a calling card of the hostel. Made in the style of the middle of the 20th century, the bar serves signature cocktails and best sorts of Belgian beer.

B&B Koetshuis
From Brugge center - 1 km

B&B Koetshuis remains one of the most secluded and romantic hotels in whole Bruges. It has only two charming guestrooms open in a wing of an old mansion, which is hidden by a lush garden from prying eyes. The hotel is designed in accordance with traditions of the past, and so it will be a wonderful destination for a romantic vacation. Every day, guests of the hotel will be able to relax in the picturesque garden in the daytime, and in the evening they are welcome at the lounge bar that serves best Belgian beer. There are many interesting sights near the hotel, including the Church of Our Lady, Minnewater Park and an ancient castle.

B&B Contrast
From Brugge center - 0.6 km

you will find B&B Contrast hotel not far from Grand Place Square, surrounded by a beautiful garden. The hotel is open in a restored single-storey building and offers only 5 comfortable guestrooms. The hotel looks very catchy because of its architectural style it feels like the hotel makes a unified whole with the nature surrounding it. Many guestrooms come with a private wooden terrace; there is also an originally looking glass covered gallery at the hotel. The garden surrounding the hotel deserves the closest attention besides interesting landscape decorations, there is a rich collection of sculptures. Some guestrooms of this unusual hotel offer charming views of the canal

Stylish Design Hotels

Stylish weekend in Brugge collection of top unique boutique hotels
B&B Lady Jane

From Brugge center - 0.7 km

Quite a small, but absolutely charming B&B Lady Jane is located in a historic building. However, its design is very stylish and far from a classic. Each guestroom comes with original individual design, but all of them are equally comfortable and will be a great choice for travelers seeking a pleasant stay in Bruges. Guests of the hotel are welcome to attend special wine and beer sampling sessions, during which they will be offered to try more than 30 sorts of finest Belgian beer, including famous Duvel, Westmalle, Karmeliet, Leffe and Hoegaarden. The sessions take place at the private wine cellar of the hotel.

Exclusive Guesthouse Bonifacius

From Brugge center - 0.4 km

Boutique hotel Exclusive Guesthouse Bonifacius is the place that fully reflects the wish of the owners to create a charming and beautiful place. Guestrooms come with antique furniture and luxurious textiles, posh decorations and genuine artworks. The roof of the building was transformed into a sunny terrace, where guests of the hotel are welcome to enjoy magnificent views of the city canals. When it's too cold to stay on the terrace, move to the warm hall with fireplace. Hospitable owner and staff of the hotel do everything to please guests and make them feel comfortable.

Montanus Hotel

From Brugge center - 0.6 km

Stylish Montanus Hotel is located right in the middle of a city park. The hotel is located in the main mansion and a smaller cottage. Travelers will be delighted with luxurious and stylish interiors that were skillfully decorated by a designer team. The 17th-century style of the white living room is worth a separate mention. Nowadays, the room was transformed into a charming bar. The peaceful atmosphere of a city park and relaxation with a cup of tea on a beautiful terrace promise travelers to be nothing but mesmerizing.

Floris Karos

From Brugge center - 0.7 km

Floris Karos is one of the newest hotels in Bruges. The charming and unforgettable architecture of the building adds to the comfort and peaceful atmosphere. Fully refurbished guestrooms of the hotel feature sophisticated and exclusive style. There is a private garden in the territory of the hotel, which is a great destination after a busy day full of sightseeing and exploration of the city. When it's cold outside, there is nothing better than to sit near the fireplace in the cozy lounge bar of the hotel.

Maison Bousson

From Brugge center - 1.2 km

Fans of modern style may be fond of Maison Bousson mini hotel. It is located not far from the centre of Bruges and is open on the site of a former quarry. The hotel has only three guest rooms made in light shades and decorated with designer furniture and interesting artworks. Besides standard paintings, one can see various colorful textiles, interesting collages, handmade items and elegant vases with flowers. The design hotel also has a wellness centre with a swimming pool.

Den Witten Leeuw

From Brugge center - 0.7 km

Many popular hotels in Bruges are located in historic buildings. Den Witten Leeuw is no exception. It is also open in an eye-catching building with centuries-old history. This hotel is very popular with couples, who enjoy staying in one of the three beautiful twin rooms with romantic design. Large white beds with canopies, posh textiles, genuine antiquities and artworks are the main design elements of this magnificent hotel. Many original decorations have been preserved in the hotel, such as historic beam joints and mansard ceilings.

Luxury Accomodations

Top places to stay in Brugge most luxury and fashionable hotels

Die Swaene

From Brugge center - 0.2 km

Die Swaene is located on a pebble pavement near a picturesque canal. The hotel is surrounded by historic buildings that only add to the heritage of the area. The main hall of Die Swaene has retained the atmosphere of the past and contains some true gems, like the elegantly painted ceiling created in 1779. Refined and luxurious guestrooms feature classic design with romantic elements and offer wonderful views of the canal. The new building of the hotel, Canal House, has some absolutely stunning guestrooms built on the sea level. Traditions and comfort of guests are highly valued at Die Swaene, so the hotel proves its respectable title of one of the most luxurious and romantic places in the city.

De Tuilerieen

From Brugge center - 0.3 km

The next hotel in our list, De Tuilerieen, enjoys an amazing location in a 15th-century mansion with an eye-catching traditional façade. Small and charming hall of the hotel is decorated with comfortable leather sofas and antiquities. It's a miracle that during its long history the hotel has retained its original atmosphere of romance and heritage. All guestrooms, big and small ones, are made in a similar style and feature mansard ceilings, arched ceiling beams and wooden floors. The hotel's bar is a no less charming place with a cozy fireplace. Owners of the hotel wanted to create historic accommodation with excellent service and its own peculiar style, and they succeeded in that.

Grand Hotel Casselbergh

From Brugge center - 0.2 km

Elegant Grand Hotel Casselbergh is located in three medieval buildings. The face of the hotel features original decorations that date back to the 13th and 16th centuries. The hotel's design is mostly classical, very elegant and contains many antique details. Luxurious rooms feature beautiful views of the canal. The hotel's lounge zone is not only a good place to pamper yourself with delicious light snacks and drinks; it's a magnificent historic place with a fireplace and a library. Fans of ultimate comfort and prestigious places will like Grand Hotel Casselbergh as it is often called the most prestigious hotel in whole Bruges.

Hotel Relais Bourgondisch Cruyce. A Luxe Worldwide Hotel

From Brugge center - 0.2 km

Absolutely marvelous Hotel Relais Bourgondisch Cruyce - A Luxe Worldwide Hotel amazes travelers right from the start the magnificent façade of this boutique hotel is made of bricks and wood and is decorated with stained-glass windows. The location of the hotel between two canals is no less amazing. Inside travelers will find luxurious textiles, elegant antiquities, and precious artworks. By the way, this hotel can be seen in the famous movie "In Bruges". Those, who have seen the movie, will surely want to visit this miraculous city and book a room at Hotel Relais Bourgondisch Cruyce.

Heritage Hotel

From Brugge center - 0.2 km

Heritage Hotel is an ultra-luxury hotel in Bruges. After a thorough restoration, an ancient mansion was turned into a hotel that deserves the highest praise. Twenty elegantly decorated rooms in mostly classic style will fit any taste and demands. Having stayed at Heritage Hotel, you will want to return there again and again!

Charming Brugge

From Brugge center - 1.2 km

Travellers, who wish to stay at an elite hotel, will like Charming Brugge mini-hotel that is located in a beautiful building constructed in 1926. This hotel has only 4 posh guestrooms with luxurious wooden décor, branded furniture and a state-of-art lighting system. Only best antique items were used in décor of public spaces. The hotel has a spa centre with sauna, massage rooms and an outdoor pool in the inner yard.

Hotels with History

Preserved history of Brugge: long-standing and historical hotels

De Orangerie

From Brugge center - 0.2 km

Spectacular De Orangerie Hotel is located in a unique historic mansion, the history of which starts yet in the 15th century. Initially, a monastery stood on the site of the mansion, in 1873 it was rebuilt into a palace. After a thorough restoration it was decided to keep the style of the 19th century, so at this hotel guests will see original marble floors, oak tree doors, skillful fretwork, genuine artworks, fine china and silver tableware of the 18th 19th centuries. The refined elegance of past centuries remains the calling card of De Orangerie.

NH Brugge

From Brugge center - 0.8 km

With its original stained-glass windows, brick fireplaces and old beam ceilings, historic NH Brugge resembles a 17th-century monastery. Guestrooms are mostly made in French countryside style. The stone terrace of the hotel is an ideal place to have a cup of coffee in the morning or relax and enjoy a delicious cocktail in the evening. The hotel's staff is very friendly, hospitable and tries to do their best to make sure guests feel comfortable and are pleased with their stay at NH Brugge.

The Pand
From Brugge center - 0.3 km

The Pand is another wonderful historic hotel, which is located in an 18th-century mansion. The family, which owns the hotel, is keen on art, so the refined taste of the owners has reflected in design and atmosphere of the hotel. Romantic guestrooms come with large beds with canopies, premium textiles, antique furniture, and are decorated with valuable artworks. A peaceful inner yard with a charming fountain, a library with a great collection of old books, a wonderful bar the atmosphere of elegance and comfort reigns throughout the hotel. On demand of travelers, fine breakfasts on silver tableware and premium champagne can be served directly in guestrooms.

Huis T Schaep
From Brugge center - 0.6 km

Huis T Schaep is located on one of the central streets in Bruges. The hotel occupies an eye-catching 17th-century building. Upon entering the hotel, you will be amazed at its unforgettable charm of the past. Guestrooms at Huis T Schaep come with posh wooden beds with high bed rests and canopies, genuine antique furniture, magnificent paintings by famous Belgian artists and other valuable and beautiful items. There is a breakfast hall on the ground floor of the building, where it's hard not to notice a marvelous buffet with antique fine china.

Vakantie Logies Hollywood
From Brugge center - 0.7 km

Vakantie Logies Hollywood is one of the most interesting historic hotels in Bruges. As it is not hard to guess from its name, the hotel's design is dedicated to Hollywood. It is located in a typical historic building with the preserved original wooden carcass. Besides antique furniture, the hotel exhibits an interesting collection of vintage photographs. In the photos, you will see Hollywood stars of the middle of the 20th century, retro filmmaking equipment and interesting on set moments. When it's warm outside, guests of this wonderful hotel are welcome to relax on an open terrace, where they will be treated with best sorts of Belgian beer.

Legendary Hotels

Brugge legends. Famous hotels glorified by history or celebrities

Relais Bourgondisch Cruyce Hotel had been a popular hotel before the famous movie "In Bruges" came out. Nowadays, one needs to book rooms in advance to be able to stay there. The wood and stone façade and large stained-glass windows of the building beautifully reflect in water of the nearby canal. All 16 guestrooms of the hotel are furnished with vintage antique items. Main characters of the movie, Ken and Ray, stayed at room 10. They considered this city a real fairy-tale, and it's hard to disagree with them. In order to reach this exceptional hotel, one needs to cross the charming Bonifacius Bridge. Upon entering the hotel, guests are greeted by the family of artist David De Graef. Travelers are offered to stay at magnificent rooms that are still reminiscent of the medieval period in the history of Bruges. The hotel is so exceptional and unique that it was selected by the family of King of Belgium, who stayed there during the honeymoon.

Kempinski Hotel Dukes Palace

From Brugge center - 0.4 km

Kempinski Hotel Dukes Palace is located in a fully restored palace of the 15th century. The palace was built by Philip the Good, the Duke of Burgundy specifically for his marriage ceremony with Isabel de Aragon. Magnificent interior of the palace is made mostly in bold violet, bronze and green shades that can be found on ancient tapestries and only underline the glorious past of the building. Gardens of the palace are no less breath-taking with their ancient sculptures by famous masters. Elegance in every detail only proves that this historic place is worth the highest praise.

Hotel Jan Brito

From Brugge center - 0.3 km

The former residence of baroness de Geiy is now known as Hotel Jan Brito. The building of the hotel is protected by UNESCO, so all restorations were very thoughtful and their main aim was to keep the original design and look of the building. Travelers are welcome to admire the beauty of antique marble fireplaces, paintings and the oak ladder. Guestrooms feature the style of different epochs, but all of them reflect the atmosphere of the past. While at the hotel, don't forget to visit a romantic inner yard of Renaissance period and a hundred-year-old beech that grows there. Despite its historic look, Hotel Jan Brito is a luxurious hotel with modern services.

Relais & Châteaux Hotel Heritage

Travellers, who find the idea of living in a hotel with rich history appealing, are recommended to pay attention to Relais & Châteaux Hotel Heritage. This hotel is located in a magnificent building constructed in 1869. Initially, the building belonged to one of rich inhabitants of Bruges. Later, the building was transformed into a bank and nowadays it's a hotel with 22 unique guestrooms that would suite even a king. Giant beds with crispy white blankets, carpets with interesting patterns, old paintings in heavy frames, crystal chandeliers you will see valuable antiques simply everywhere in this amazing hotel. By the way, there is a 14th-century wine cellar at the hotel, which has survived from the original building.

Romantic Hotels

Brugge for couples in love best hotels for intimate escape, wedding or honeymoon

Relais Bourgondisch Cruyce

From Brugge center - 0.2 km

Let yourself be charmed by the most romantic hotel in Europe. Relais Bourgondisch Cruyce is elegantly decorated with valuable antiquities, exclusive artworks, premium furniture and magnificent flower bouquets. The hotel offers simply mesmerizing views of the historic city centre and will help you enjoy an absolutely unforgettable vacation in the magic city of Bruges.

Jacquemine Luxury Guesthouse and Art Gallery

From Brugge center - 0.4 km

Jacquemine Luxury Guesthouse and Art Gallery offers travellers to stay in romantic and elegant guestrooms with beautiful design, in which guests will find a comfortable leather sofa, flat TV, teapots and a coffee machine. The hotel is surrounded by a charming Japanese garden that borders with a canal. This is a fantastic choice for a great family weekend!

Maison Bousson

From Brugge center - 1.2 km

Located in a peaceful area, Maison Bousson is a small boutique hotel with beautifully decorated elegant rooms, which are nothing but perfect for a romantic vacation. Various facilities, such as an outdoor swimming pool, will make your stay at Maison Bousson very comfortable. Active travellers are offered to make a bicycle ride in the hotel's garden. When it's cold outside, there's nothing better than to relax in a cozy hall near the fireplace. The atmosphere of calmness, peace and comfort will surround you during your stay at romantic Bruges.

Brugsche Suites - Luxury Guesthouse

From Brugge center - 1 km

Brugsche Suites - Luxury Guesthouse is a charming mansion that has only three stylish suites. The rooms feature all modern amenities including a spacious bathroom and a living room with a fireplace. Decorated with antique furniture, the suites have the charm and appeal of a rich house. The hospitable atmosphere and luxurious furnishing of this high-class guesthouse will please even most discerning travellers. Brugsche Suites - Luxury Guesthouse will be a perfect choice for travellers who seek serene and calm pastime.

Martins Relais

From Brugge center - 0.4 km

Couples, who are used to staying in high-class hotels, may like Martins Relais. This luxurious hotel is located near a canal and occupies a complex of five fully restored historic buildings that were constructed more than 300 years ago. At the hotel, travellers will find amazing posh guestrooms decorated with antique furniture and retro textiles. Without a doubt, suites are the most romantic place at Martins Relais as they feature charming views of the canal. There is a cozy bar with an amazing choice of cocktails and signature drinks at the hotel. However, travellers are not limited to facilities present at the hotel as only a short walk separates them from the Market Square and central streets.

Casa Romantico

From Brugge center - 0.4 km

Villa-hotel Casa Romantico is an ideal place for couples who seek privacy and serenity. This hotel is also open in a beautiful historic building and is surrounded by a lush garden. Besides charming guestrooms, guests of the hotel are welcome to rest in a cozy inner yard with wooden terraces and an outdoor swimming pool. The guestrooms look slightly different, but all of them feature beautiful handmade wooden furniture and premium textiles. The most unusual room is located on the mansard and has beautiful beam ceiling. Finally, there is a nice bar at the hotel, which is a great place in the evening.

Things to do

The Venice of the North: The city by boat

Many European cities with canals Amsterdam, sometimes even Manchester and Liverpool are described as the 'Venice of the North'. It's not true of those places, but it is true of Bruges. The best way to see the city is to find someone with a private boat to take you around. Setting out first thing in the morning, especially on an autumn or winter day, when you might get some atmospheric fog on the water, you can almost fool yourself into feeling that you are journeying back into the past. On my last visit, I was taken around by an off-duty fireman; in Bruges they travel to fires by boat and then pump water from the canal to put out the blaze, so a fireman needs a boat licence. Travelling the canals, you see the way the city's architecture is orientated towards the water, and only by doing that can you really understand the miracle that Bruges is.

The whole of the Low Countries Belgium, the Netherlands, Luxembourg represents a miracle of human ingenuity over a hostile environment. In many places the sea level is higher than that of flat land, so the fact that it was drained in the 11th and 12th centuries to an extent that cities thrive is a great achievement. In Belgium, there are weird relationships between land and water you'll be driving along a road and suddenly realise you're going under a canal. But the advantage for the Belgians, having created cities like Bruges, Ghent and Antwerp, is that they were all connected by this network of waterways. For example, it's an easy four-mile cycle along the canal from Bruges to its pretty neighbouring port of Damme. Because these waterways were the arteries of trade, Bruges became rich during the Middle Ages and the Renaissance.

On the canals, you realise that the houses don't face the water because it's pretty, but because that's where business is. Bruges' prime businesses, such as brewing and textiles, which reached their zenith in the 14th century, were made possible by manipulating water. That's why Belgium has the best and most varied beer, because they have so much water. The monasteries, in particular, were very good at harnessing fresh water. Drink a beer in Bruges and you are actually touching history, as those brewing traditions are as ancient as the city itself. Drink several beers, especially strong ones like Leffe or Pelforth, and you might end up forgetting history altogether, including your own!

The land around Bruges wasn't fertile, and people couldn't live on fish alone, so they produced things; beer and textiles like their famous lace, which could be transported along the canal network. Canals, towpaths, horses pulling barges this was all cutting-edge technology, developed in Belgium and later taken up everywhere else. And that's why Bruges is such a magnificent city, it was created by sheer force of will. On the canals it's possible to feel all that, and it's simultaneously a very peaceful way to see the city. Bruges is a touristy place and can feel crowded, but on the water you're removed from the hustle and bustle. Travel along the Groenerei, or Green Canal, and you might even spot Bruges' most famous dog: a Labrador who sits up in a beautiful Renaissance window, watching the world go by.

Bruges business: The city's ancient markets

Within Belgium, the Brugeoise have a reputation for being greedy and rapacious. Hardly very surprising when their city was built on business; their essence was to market. The heart of the city is Markt, a beautiful open market square. It's surrounded by gabled medieval buildings and the former market halls. The old stone slabs which traders used to cut and sell meat and other produce, like cloth, have been preserved. Looming over it all is the Belfort, the city's 13th-century belfry the scene of a particularly dramatic moment in the film *In Bruges*. In a place as flat as Belgium, the only way to get a view to really get a sense of the lie of the land and see how the city works is to get up high. From the top of the tower you look down on to a web of canals, on to the little roof terraces that the people of the city are so fond of cultivating, and out across the flat landscape towards distant wind farms.

Around the corner, Bruges' fabulous fish market is still very much a working market. The Brugeoise December 2012 Lonely Planet Traveller 83 love their fish; fresh, raw herring is the Belgian equivalent of Japanese sushi, and highly prized. Every summer, the first barrel of herring to be caught enough for, say, 100 people to eat is sold at auction and traditionally goes for around €70,000. The winning bid is given to charity, so it's a big prestige thing among the benevolent super-rich.

A great delicacy, herring is eaten with raw onions and gherkin. A really nice thing to do is to stop at the fish market, buy a load of herring and make yourself a little picnic, with a couple of bottles of Belgian beer. Again, with a meal like this you're eating the history of this place, because herring was traditionally what local people lived on; it's how human habitation was even possible in this cold, wet place, before the city became rich. The Romans called the Belgians a 'miserable tribe of herringeating primitives', but the Belgians had the last laugh when they created Bruges.

Rich in oil: Bruges on canvas

During the 15th century Bruges became a centre for a stunningly new and completely beguiling artistic technique: oil painting. Its great masters were Jan van Eyck and Rogier van der Weyden, and their work can be seen at Bruges' Groeningemuseum. It isn't a huge gallery but its collection is spectacular. It has the wonderful *Madonna with Canon van der Paele* by Jan van Eyck a frozen, seated Madonna with a Bruges clergyman kneeled beside her. At the same time this was painted, 1436, the Italians were using fresco, painting murals on freshly laid plaster. It gives vivid images but not the sense that you can actually touch someone's arm or see the moistness in the corner of their eye as with oil.

Oil paint's potential was discovered in Flanders in the 1430s. We're not sure how it was discovered, but it completely transformed the whole history of western art. Perhaps because the Low Countries' culture came from a world of near nothingness, derided by the ancient Romans as a watery wilderness, they loved art that was rich. In Flemish painting you get everything gold, silver, jewels; the Madonna wearing something beautiful; castles in the landscape. Artists stacked up visual elements for the viewer to enjoy. At the time, people were so stunned by the hypnotic realism of oil painting they put it about that Jan van Eyck had sold his soul to the devil for the ability to paint like that. It's impossible for us now to understand its impact. Imagine a world with no advertisements, no photographs, no cars. You go to church and see an altarpiece that is almost photographically real it must have been astonishing.

A lot of the Groeningemuseum's great works were once in the city's churches and cathedrals. Hugo van der Goes' *St Hippolyte Triptych* was restored by the museum, but is now back in its original home, St Saviour's Cathedral. The painting is a transfixing and completely weird depiction of a saint about to be torn in four by men on horseback. The scene is painted within an inviting landscape, and there's this beautiful sky in the background. It's odd and makes you ask how something so horrible could be happening in such a peaceful place. Another one of my favourites is *Death and the Miser*, by Jan Provoost. It's a fantastic picture of a Flemish Scrooge-character being paid a final visit by a skeletal Death. In the background are bottle glass windows, still seen in Bruges today.

There was a tendency among Bruges' painters to set everything in the present day in their own world. For example, you might be looking at a painting of the nativity story, and the Holy Family will be wandering not through Bethlehem but Bruges. It'll be a Bruges innkeeper saying, 'Sorry, no room at the inn,' and there'll be a dog barking at them from the doorstep of a little gabled house. Because Bruges has been so carefully preserved as a medieval city, when you're walking its streets you can feel like you're walking within these paintings. Particularly at night, when the streets tend to be emptier of day-tripping tourists in the semidarkness, the illusion is more convincing.

A place of pilgrimage: The St-Janshospitaal

You can really sense the city's past at St-Janshospitaal, a 12th-century hospital building which is a wonderful mix of Flanders' Middle Ages culture. Now a museum, it's a reminder that although the canals were good for business, they also brought the plague to the city, and the way Bruges ministered to their sick was through religion. The hospital's chapel was a pilgrimage site. It held the relics of St Ursula, a virgin killed by Huns people around the 4th or 5th century while returning from a pilgrimage to Rome.

In the 15th century, the hospital commissioned the artist Hans Memling to create a shrine for the relics. Memling was described by the art historian Erwin Panofsky as 'the very model of a major minor master', which is a highbrow joke taken from Gilbert and Sullivan's operas. In other words, he was the perfect second-rate artist. But his shrine really is wonderful, bridging the gap between the medieval foundations of the hospital and its Renaissance incarnation. Memling took the old reliquary containing Ursula's remains a wooden box, which people had been coming to touch for hundreds of years and then housed it in a sort of dolls' house in the shape of a miniature church. On this he painted the whole story of Ursula's journey: her life and death.

Flemish oil painting was born out of manuscript illumination, of which Bruges was a great centre. Walking around Memling's shrine, it's clear to see how one gave rise to the other. It's a bit like the pages of a story book, put onto the outside of a box. It's no surprise that Belgium also produced the artist and comics writer Hergé; Memling's box is almost like a Renaissance Tintin tale, unfolding frame by frame. Ursula even dies being watched by her little dog, like a mournful little Snowy. The paintings are full of such wonderful details. The pope, as well as looking serious, receiving all these virgins in Rome, has the appearance of a naughty schoolboy. The characters are wearing these fantastically fine fabrics, so even when you're watching Ursula being killed, you're also checking out what she's wearing. Narratively, this isn't terribly convincing but it is very revealing of the contemporary culture.

Hans Memling knew perfectly well that people would come from far and wide to be in the presence of Ursula's reliquary. This shrine was a big tourist attraction, drawing people to Bruges. So he made it an advert for what the city had to offer. It was saying: 'Come on a pilgrimage, say your prayers, let's hope that your husband recovers from his illness. And before you leave, why don't you do a bit of shopping?' In the art of Flanders especially the Renaissance art, which I love there's this wonderful collision between spirituality and materialism. They want their art to be deeply spiritual, absolutely, but it's also a way of stocking the world with riches.

Minnewater Lake

Located just south of the De Halve Maan Brewery, Minnewater Lake (which literally means "Lake of Love") is a charming body of water bookended by canals. There are park benches, weeping willows, walking paths and even swans that give the lake a lovely ambience. Some say the canalized lake is best viewed in autumn, when the willow leaves change color.

Most people agree that the Minnewater Lake is a must-see for its romantic atmosphere and pleasant views. However, some visitors weren't impressed, like this user who says, "It's a pleasant enough stretch of water with nice paths and seats but I wouldn't fight my way past all the other things in Bruges to go there." Visitors also mention that there are a few good restaurants skirting the lake, one of which sells tasty waffles.

Historic Centre of Brugge

Since 2000, the Historic Centre of Brugge has been a UNESCO World Heritage Site for its "outstanding example of a medieval historic settlement, which has maintained its historic fabric as this has evolved over the centuries." Canals or cobblestone paths frame these medieval buildings (and gothic ones too), giving the area an old world feel. These restored buildings once housed merchants selling leather, fish and more. Now, the historic buildings are repurposed as cafés, boutiques and art galleries. One tourist exclaims that the Historic Centre of Brugge is a must-see, citing the local food and shops. You'll find this neighborhood right in the center of Bruges, roughly encircled by the Ring Canal.

De Halve Maan Brewery

Bruges once contained dozens of breweries, but now De Halve Maan is the last one standing. With a history that dates back to the 16th century, the brewery has been continuously operating at its current site since 1856. Today, visitors can tour the historic facility, get some great photos from its tower and sample the beer.

An Asian tourst says, "The brewery tour is nice, the view of the city from the roof is great, but the beer is the BEST part!" And a Virtual Tourist user gives specific beer recommendations: "The drink at the brewery, Straffe Hendrike or 'Strong Henry' is really good. Ask for the light beer or the 'Blonde. Atourist describes this blonde as having a "clean, heavenly taste." However, some say the Brugse Zot is the way to go.

Brewery tours last about 45 minutes and cost €6 EUR (a little more than $8 USD) per person. You'll find it south of the Historic Centre of Brugge on Walplein.

Markt

Tourists calls the Markt, the "nerve center" of Bruges. And you can see why: Shadowed by medieval buildings, the area is peppered with cafés that spill out into the streets. Horse-drawn carriages also clip-clop through the city square. And did we mention tourists? There are almost always a ton of those too. You'll find it right in the heart of Bruges, within a five or six-minute walk from the Church of Our Lady and the Groeninge Museum.

A travler describes the Markt like this: "Lovely square ... many historic buildings with loads of small side roads with loads of pubs/bars!" But this user (and many others) recommend bringing plenty of money, saying this is one of the most expensive areas of the small city.

The Lucifernum

This former Masonic lodge has been transformed into part museum, part bar, all awesome.

While The Lucifernum in Bruges, Belgium is the

private home of Barnum-esque provocateur Don

"Willy" Retsin, the local celebrity often opens the doors of his repurposed Masonic Lodge to wild parties among the strange portraits and curious artifacts he has accumulated. Thanks to him and his Peruvian wife, who you are surely to meet once inside, a truly interesting combination of live performance and libation awaits.

As Retsin, a self-described "vampire," describes it, his house originally housed a chapter of the Freemasons during the time of Napoleon. However during his residence in the space, he has refurbished the rich interior to resemble a living cabinet of curiosities. The walls are covered in huge portraits of vaguely sinister figures like something out of a particularly ominous nightmare, and the surfaces are covered in countless statues and figures that seem to have been collected from a wide range of eras and areas (and possibly horror dimensions). Retsin himself consideres the space to act as a sort of museum.

There is also a distinctly Cuban flavor to much of the space and the events inside with rich rum cocktails served from the old bar and Latin music playing. This owes to Retsin's professed past of textile trading in Central America. Regardless of the origins, the sense of Havana nights decadence pervades the home although it has been filtered through the morbid sensibility of a living oddity/most interesting man in the world.

Today The Lucifernum is open to the public on Sundays from 8 p.m to 11p.m. when daring party animals can ring the bell and be welcomed into the vampire's lair.

Basilica of the Holy Blood

Christ's blood preserved in a Belgian town.

The Basilica of the Holy Blood (Basiliek van het Heilig Bloed) is a 12th century chapel, in the medieval town of Bruges, Belgium, which houses a revered vial containing cloth stained with the actual blood of Christ. Or so it is believed.

While the chapel itself is a beautiful site, it is the blood and its accompanying story that attracts visitors, from the devoutly religious to the deeply skeptical to those just curious to know what the fuss is all about.

It is popular legend that following the Crucifixion, Joseph of Arimathea wiped blood from the body of Christ and the cloth was preserved. The artifact was kept safe in the Holy Land until the time of the Second Crusade when King of Jerusalem Baldwin III gave it to his brother-in-law, Count of Flanders Diederik van de Elzas. The Count then took the relic back to Bruges where it sits in the upper chapel of the Basilica, still unopened to this day. The vial itself is a marvel, adorned with gold and enclosed at each end by coronets decorated with angels. The chapel is open daily to visitors who wish to view the relic.

On Ascension Day, a festival known as the Procession of the Holy Blood attracts residents and tourists alike. It is on this day that the Bishop of Bruges carries the cherished vial through the streets preceded by residents performing an historic reenactment of the relic's arrival and acting out other biblical scenes. The first recorded procession took place in 1291, and some 718 years later, it is still happening.

Lumina Domestica

Explore 400,000 years of humans' "battle against darkness" in this offbeat but thorough lamp museum.

Some of Bruges' most trafficked and hackneyed tourist destinations are museums about the most iconic Belgian foods: fries and chocolate. While those museums appeal to the masses, their sister museum is dedicated to a more esoteric though no less important topic: lamps.

The most endearing thing about Lumina Domestica (The Lamp Museum) is that it truly feels like the passion project of a devoted collector. The collection features a staggering array of more than 6,000 lamps, though it doesn't display all of them at once.

According to the museum, its exhibits show visitors all aspects of the "more than 400,000 years of humans' battle against darkness."

The museum has items spanning from the earliest prehistoric clay lamps to oil lamps that look like they're holding a genie inside to much more recognizable modern examples. These artifacts are accompanied by a bevy of text and video explaining more about the history of lamps, focusing primarily on indoor lighting.

Smedenpoort Skull

The bronzed skull of a beheaded traitor was affixed to the city gate in the 17th century.

The medieval Smedenpoort, or "Blacksmith's Gate," dates back to 1297, and is one of the four remaining city gates of Bruges. Look closely at the upper lefthand corner above the arch and you'll notice a morbid curiosity: A bronzed human skull is affixed to the gate's yellow brick facade.

It is a replica of the skull of an executed traitorous statesman whose head was prominently displayed as a warning to the people. In 1691, hostile French troops had gathered near Bruges but could not infiltrate the city's ramparts. They conspired with Belgian statesman François van der Straeten to enter the city through the Smedenpoort.

Unfortunately for the conspirators, the plot was discovered and relayed to the city council. François van der Straeten was arrested on June 26, 1691, and hanged. His head was dipped in bronze and then hung from an iron pin on the gate as *exemplum justitiae.*

The skull disappeared during the French Revolution and was rediscovered in 1876. The remnants of the original skull are housed in the Archaeological Museum in Bruges, and a bronze replica now hangs on the Smedenpoort.

Know Before You Go
The gate that stands today was rebuilt in 1367 in place of the original 1297 gate. It has been restored several times over the centuries. The

skull that hangs on the gate is a replica of the original.

The Smedenpoort is located on the edge of the west side of the city. The other western gate, Ezelpoort, is about 2 kilometers away. The other two original gates are located on the eastern side of town: Kruispoort, at Langestraat 191, and Gentpoort at Gentpoortstraat.

Halve Maan Brewery Beer Pipeline

A beer pipeline runs beneath Bruges.
Running underneath the city streets of the medieval city of Bruges is a contemporary innovation: a pipeline for beer. The tube transports 1,000 gallons of beer per hour the equivalent of 12,000 bottles from one of the country's oldest still-operational breweries, Halve Maan ("half moon"), to its bottling plant two miles away.

Brouwerij De Halve Maan opened in Bruges in 1856. A century and a half later, in 2016, a crowdsourcing campaign was launched to raise funds for the beer pipeline. The 500+ donors received a priceless thank you gift: free beer for life. Today, visitors can glimpse a section of the pipeline through a transparent manhole cover cut into the cobblestone street.

There are other, older beer pipelines that set the precedent for this one in Bruges. In 1930, a 6,000-foot-long hose was discovered under the streets of Yonkers, New York, which is believed to have been a conduit for beer during Prohibition. There are also underground pipes between the breweries in Munich and Theresienwiese, where the Oktoberfest takes place.

The Procession of the Holy Blood

This gruesome biblical parade celebrates the one day a year that a bit of Jesus' blood turns to liquid.

Each year, forty days after the Easter holiday, the largest procession in the city of Bruges, Belgium takes to the streets to parade around a vial of what is said to be the blood of Jesus Christ so that it might once again become liquid for a time.

The Procession of the Holy Blood, also known as the "Most Beautiful Day in Bruges," has been taking place each year since the 13th century when the relic is said to have come to the city. As the story goes it was brought to Bruges after the Second Crusade, and on the Thursday that falls 40 days after Easter, the otherwise dried blood becomes wet once more. The revery was created to celebrate this miracle.

Over 3,000 participants march in the parade each year in various costumes and roles. There are a number of Bible stories that are represented with people dressed as pilgrims and pharaohs, as well as a menagerie of beasts ranging from camels to donkeys. In addition to all of the recreations, a large number of the marchers are actual church officials including the 30-strong Brotherhood of the Holy Blood who look after the reliquary. Filled out with floats, bands, choirs, and other solemn revelers, the parade is an unrivaled spectacle, save when the actual blood passes the crowd at which point the air turns quiet and reverent.

Anywhere from 60,000 to 100,000 people come from all over the world to witness the holy parade each year and the practice itself has received UNESCO protected status. Not bad for a little spilt blood.

Frietmuseum

Potato-peeling mannequins, Inca art, and a dangling tuber mobile help trace the history of fries at this Belgian museum.

In Bruges, nestled among the Gothic architecture and outdoor cafes dolling out beer and waffles, lies the world's only museum dedicated to fries.

While some might call fried potatoes "French" fries, it's well known that Belgium is the real source of *pommes frites*, and the Frietmuseum pays tribute to this national cuisine. Inside a 14th-century building known as the Saaihalle, founders Cédric and Eddy Van Belle have assembled a curious collection of artifacts, equipment, and art. Their museum traces the history of the fry, from Andean potatoes to Belgium's iconic paper cones of crispy, hot pommes frites. There's an Inca-era vase featuring potatoes, dioramas of Peruvian farmers and potato-peeling European soldiers, vintage ads, an extensive assortment of potato cutters, and a mobile of dangling tubers of various hues and sizes from around the world.

After working up an appetite, visitors can descend to the medieval cellar, where a cafe dishes up pommes frites, among other items such as croquettes and beef stew.

Know Before You Go

The Frietmuseum is open every day from 10:00 a.m. to 5:00 p.m. (last tickets at 4.15 p.m.). Entry costs $8 (7€) per adult.

Secret Garden of Bruges

You would never come across this tiny green oasis if you didn't know it existed. *People come from all over the world to the medieval city of Bruges for the amazing architecture, delicious beer and tasty chocolate, but not many know about this little secret garden that is hidden in one of the tiny alleys, away from the main touristic route but still right in the city center.*

The story of the garden like most stories in Bruges is not known exactly. But it is believed that the once-abandoned house where the garden grows never got renovated, and thus stood roofless and rundown much to the chagrin of the residents on the block. So neighbors around started using the ruins as an extra space for a bunch of different plants and herbs, which grew into a beautiful public kitchen garden.

Here you can find, for example, mint, thyme, basil, wild strawberries and some exotic trees. The plants are labeled and there are quotes written along the walls of the whimsical community garden. The place itself is tiny, but definitely worth the extra stroll

Things you absolutely must-do in Bruges

The comely city we see today took shape in the 15th century - the 'Golden Age' - when the Royal House of Burgundy established residence here, and its churches and merchant houses were built. The best way to discover this World Heritage Site is on foot and there are plenty of great things to do along the way.

Climb the Belfry of Bruges

The best views of Bruges are to be enjoyed from the top of Belfry in The Market Square, the 900-year-old beating heart of the city. The colourful guild houses and clatter of horses hooves make for a picturesque setting but the daddy on the square is the 13th-century Belfry standing at a vertigo-inducing 83 metres high.

Anyone fit enough is obliged to climb the building's 366 steps to the bell tower whose carillon houses 47 melodious bells, the largest of which dates from 1680, is two metres in diameter and weighs six tonnes. Don't forget the cotton wool buds.

The Witches exhibition at Musea Bruges
You'll be familiar with the Flemish renaissance artist Pieter Bruegel the Elder from paintings such as The Hunters In The Snow and Netherlandish Proverbs, but did you know that this was the artist who first depicted witches flying out of chimneys on broomsticks and toothless hags huddled around bubbling cauldrons? Prototypes that endure to this day.

The story goes in 1565, a time when witch hunts were rife in Europe, an Antwerp printmaker by the name of Hieronymous Cock issued two prints by Bruegel: Saint James At The Sorcerer's Den and Saint James And The Fall Of The Sorcerer. All manner of creeps and weird mutations populate these prints and they set the trend for other artists during this period of religious hysteria.

In addition to other Bruegel works, the show also features splendidly diabolical oils by lesser lights such David Teniers II, Leonaert Bramer and Cornelis Saftleven, films and installations. The exhibition ends on June 26.

The gruesomeness continues at the Torture Museum Oude Steen (old stone) on Wollestraat, the plot of one of oldest prisons in Europe. Here, an alarming array of sadistic contraptions (don't worry, they're replicas), mostly from medieval times, can be enjoyed by all the family. Free jelly tots on entry.

Art in abundance

For its size Bruges contains an inordinate amount of art galleries and museums, from local art to collections dedicated to the likes Of Salvador Dali and Picasso.

The Groeningemuseum is the place to see the Flemish Primitives, artists of the so-called Northern Renaissance of the 14th to 16th centuries.

Here you find Hans Memling's Moreel Triptych (1484), and The Virgin And Child With Canon Van der Paele by Jan van Eyck, an extraordinary feat of fine detail and spacial complexity that took two years to complete. Van Eyck's brother Hubert painted one of the greatest works of all time, The Ghent Altarpiece or Adoration Of The Mystic Lamb (1432), a 12-panel work intended as an altarpiece for the chapel in the former church of St John, now Bavo's Catherdral. Over the centuries the hapless work has been robbed by Napoleon, burned by Calvinists, hidden in a salt mine and coveted by the Nazis.

But it is a beautiful thing and certainly warrants a trip to Ghent..

Expo Picasso in Bruges is also worth a visit and can be found in the former hospital of Saint John, where more than 300 works reside by the Spanish artist from Surrealist and Cubist works to engravings, drawings and ceramics.

The canal trip
A very agreeable half an hour should be spent travelling the cities arteries where secret gardens, picturesque bridges and crumbly old houses look even more beautiful when viewed from the water.

Bruges has a mild maritime climate and summer is warm without being unpleasantly hot, perfect conditions for the canal tour.

Eat your heart out

For good quality and inexpensive dining, few European cities can rival Bruges. Mussels and chips of course is a staple, but this might be eaten away from the Market Square where I found the view failed to compensate for the much heavier bill.

Along the streets off the market, fabulous little eateries await you.

The Bistro De Pompe, for example, on Kleine Sint-Amandsstraat 2, is a very cosy space with decor that reminded me of 1970s sitcom Robin's Nest, with wine baskets, thickly upholstered seating and a dessert trolley.

My delicious lunch of herring, a local beef stew and apple tart came in at 16 euros, drinks not included. Another find was Brasserie Lumiere in the pretty Beguinage area, not far from the Hotel Montanus, my place of repose. The menu mixes north African and classic European dishes and surely cannot be beaten for value. I must have supped on the best nine-Euro bouillabaisse in the world.

The most interesting dining took place at Kok au Vin at Ezelstraat 21, where a French/Belgian menu flirts with global cuisine, and with chefs, I was assured, who improvise as spontaneously as possible on a day to day basis. My egg cup of pork pate with fresh cheese and radish coolie and sea bass marinated "South American" style with grapes, walnuts and pomegranates were truly humbling.

Another first was a glass of prosecco mixed with a soda of bergamot, which clouded the wine and gave it both a smokiness and creaminess.

Relax in the Beguinage
This is a little haven of tranquility where swans gather on the banks of the canal and people relax in the pretty restaurants and bars that line the perimeter.

The Beguinage became popular in Flemish kingdom of the 14th century and were semi-monastic dwellings for women, where the way of life was similar to that of a convent, but the women never took oaths.

It's beer o'clock
And so to beer. Of the countless brews on offer I could have contented myself sipping the weighty but floral Tripel Karmeliet (8.4%) for the duration of my stay, but I felt a visit to at least one brewery was in order. De Halve Maan (Half Man)

brewery is where the excellent Zot is made, Bruges's city beer.

The family business stretches back six generations to 1856 and is the only remaining family-fun brewery in the centre of the city. Brugse Zot is a strong malt-based beer that is found everywhere. There is a dark and blonde version and visitors are treated to a glass of the latter at the end of the 45-minute tour.

Keep tabs on the bars
Beer enthusiasts should prioritise two places: T'Brugs Beertje and Cambrinus - the former boasts around Belgian 300 brews while that latter has more than 400, even if you don't drink, the colourful array of bottles and pumps are beautiful to behold.

Vino Vino and Bar Salon both serve hearty tapas dishes and the latter doubles as a hipster hang out. There's a great buzz in Charlie Rockets, an old cinema, that's popular with backpackers, especially during happy hour, and the pool table is big hit too.

Check out Choco-Story (The Chocolate Museum)
The story of chocolate is related from the Maya and the Spanish conquistadores right up to today's craft culture.

Children can learn about the sweet stuff by taking part in a chocolate hunt and the making of chocs by hand can be observed on the premises and then the goods can be sampled.

Drawn by horse and carriage
At 50 euros per carriage the tour is a little on the dear side, so try and get the maximum of five passengers for the best deal. The ride through some of Bruges' oldest streets lasts for 30 minutes and the driver provides captivating

commentary. Carriages depart from the Market Square.

Momentous Historical Sites in Belgium

Squeezed between traditional military powerhouses Germany and France, Belgium has seen more than its fair share of battlefields and wartime curiosities. Combined with a medieval town straight out of a storybook and the ancient cathedral that houses one of the most coveted artworks of all time, these five historic sites show that the small country at the heart of Europe has played an essential role in the continent's history.

Waterloo, where Napoleon met his match

In an all-or-nothing clash on the fields of Waterloo, about 30 kilometers (18.6 miles) south of Brussels, Napoleon's troops met a coalition of

British, German, Dutch and Belgian forces on June 18, 1815. Eight hours later, the business was finished. In a crushing victory that was accomplished mainly due to good timing Marshal von Blücher's Prussian forces dealt a painful blow to Napoleon's right flank at a pivotal moment the international alliance led by the Duke of Wellington put an end to the French domination of Europe and installed a period of relative peace that would last almost a decade. Today, a monumental lion statue stands proud on its mound in the middle of the battlefield. Audio guides and tours deliver more insight into one of the last close quarters military battles waged on the continent.

Bruges's city center, Belgium's storybook medieval town

A regular on best-preserved European cities lists, Bruges's town core has slept straight through modern times. Having been a wealthy merchant harbor in the middle ages, its step-gabled houses, winding canals, and imposing Belfry all escaped the talons of modernization after its lifeline river silted up during the 15th century. Three centuries later, British travelers, who were making their way to Waterloo, rediscovered the sleepy town, and the entire center became a UNESCO World Heritage Site in 2000.

Plugstreet, site of a wartime Christmas miracle

As far as the countless war memorials spread throughout Belgium go, the Plugstreet football is decidedly more cheerful than most. The simple monument, a soccer ball perched on a rust-colored pedestal, remembers something of a Christmas miracle. On the eve of December 24, 1914, over 100,000 soldiers from both sides of the Western Front emerged from their muddy trenches, white flags waving, and proceeded to celebrate Christmas together by way of carols and a soccer game. Belgium saw one of the most famed of these jovial truces take place in the tiny Walloon town of Ploegsteert "Plugstreet" to the Britons and memories of this particular game have gone into plenty of soldiers' diaries. Helmets served as makeshift goalposts, Scots played in kilts with nothing underneath, and English whisky was traded for German sausage in what Sir Arthur Conan Doyle has called a "human episode amid all the atrocities which have stained the memory of war."

The Menin Gate, a daily tribute

As the unfortunate Belgian region had to endure four years of muddy trench warfare during World War I, the Ypres Salient is dotted with monuments dedicated to the more than half a million soldiers who lost their lives in Flanders' no man's land. Among these, the Menin Gate, with its moving Last Post Ceremony, is one of the most important. Every evening since 1928, local buglers have sounded their instruments underneath the Hall of Memory at 8 p.m. sharp. After, the fourth verse of Laurence Binyon's poem for the Fallen is read aloud, fittingly ending on "we will remember them." The minute of silence that follows can't help but emphasize the power of this daily ritual.

Saint Bavo's Cathedral, home to the world's most stolen artwork

Stolen a record 13 times by looting armies and art-hungry Nazis among others, *The Adoration of the Mystic Lamb* didn't win the title of "world's most coveted artwork" lightly. Now hanging safe and sound inside Ghent's Saint Bavo's Cathedral, its original home since 1432, the 12-panel altarpiece by Renaissance brothers Hubert and

Jan van Eyck has traveled more than most people will in a lifetime.

Being one of the first large-scale oil paintings ever made and one depicting Catholic mythicism in breathtaking detail, the artwork's reputation soon spread far and wide over the continent. Over the course of six centuries, it was taken by Napoleonic troops, a mischievous Ghent vicar, Nazis and eventually the Monuments Men, who were the last to return it to its rightful home over 60 years ago. Meanwhile, Ghent's Saint-Bavo's Cathedral had become an esteemed holder of other religious art as well, including an altarpiece by Rubens and a celebrated Rococo pulpit.

Architectural tour of Bruges' Gothic Landmarks

When it comes to brick or Brabantine Gothic, architectural movements that flourished in

Northern Europe in the Middle Ages, the idyllic Belgian city of Bruges paints a comprehensive picture. Its UNESCO-listed old town core, having mostly slept through the Industrial Revolution, is still rich with well-preserved authentic gems in this style, as well as plenty of its 19th-century disciples. We take you on a tour of the most characterful Gothic buildings in Bruges.

Basilica of the Holy Blood: Eye-catching because of its flamboyant Renaissance façade and at the same time tucked away in one corner of the Burg Square, the Basilica of the Holy Blood actually consists of two very different chapels. While the lower is Romanesque and modest in appearance, the dazzling upper chapel equals full-on Gothic extravagance. It is here, amid splendid colours, ornate altars and religiously themed art, that Bruges' most precious relic is brought out for lengthy veneration twice a day. The crystal vial with a stained piece of cloth in it is believed to hold the blood of Jesus Christ, brought back from the Second Crusade by the Count of Flanders in the 12th century.

City Hall: Already confirming that Bruges has Gothic landmarks galore, the Basilica of the Holy Blood's neighbour to the left is City Hall, one of the oldest town halls of the Lower Countries. Its eggshell façade boasts statuettes of Flanders' counts and countesses, ornate little arches, and a general lavishness that has made it an excellent example of the late Gothic style also known to awe beholders of Leuven's and Brussels' mayoral seats. Inside resides a shining star in the neo-Gothic department: the polychrome vaulted ceiling of the 'Gothic Hall', an exquisite room that includes historic murals to daydream about, painted in the Romantic 19th century. This particular gem came from the mind of city architect and noted Gothic revivalist Louis Delacenserie, who played a major role in returning Bruges to its former Gothic glory as the end of the 19th century approached.

Belfry: Master of the Bruges skyline and former regulator of town life thanks to its impressive bell collection (once described by poet Henry Wadsworth Longfellow as 'a heart of iron beating in the ancient tower'), the Belfry sits on the Markt. Originally built in the 13th century but consumed by fire and lightning no less than three times, it sits atop the old market hall, which is why locals also know it by the name 'Halletoren'. Conquering its narrow, 366-step staircase has become somewhat of a badge of honour among travellers. While waiting to climb all the way to its octagonal lantern tower of sand-lime brick in High Gothic style, the tower's survivor story can be soaked up in its reception area.

The Church of Our Lady: Reaching to the sky for over 122 metres (400 feet), the Church of Our Lady's spire qualifies as the largest brickwork tower in the world. It's widely seen as the testament to the excellence of Bruges' artisan stonemasons, partly thanks to its tasteful mix of the evolving Gothic styles a necessity given the two centuries it took to erect the religious abode. A central nave, built in 1225, features Tournai stone in the Scheldt style, while the choirs and portals were constructed using the later, popular French and Brabantine variants. Add to that the only Michelangelo statue that ever left Italy during the artist's lifetime (a Madonna and Child in white Carrara marble), the tombstones of Mary of Burgundy and her father Charles the Bold with beautiful bronze effigies, and paintings by local Flemish primitives such as Pieter Poubus and Gerard David, and you've got a beautiful Gothic frame with a grand art inner sanctum.

Gruuthuse Museum: This splendid city palace just behind the Church of Our Lady spent a surprising stint as a pawn shop. It was a peculiar period between its original role as the home to the rich and powerful Lords of Gruuthuse, a family that thrived in the merchant town thanks to its control over the wheat trade, and its current status as a city museum. Currently closed for extensive restorations but aiming to reopen by 2018, the palace holds an eclectic selection of applied and decorative arts. On its prior refurbishment, which rounded up in 1898, it was again Louis Delacenserie who took the lead, and this building too received a certain neo-Gothic flair in the process.

The Burgher's Lodge: In the same category of legendary hubs of power and wealth, we find the early 15th-century 'Poortersloge', or Burgher's Lodge. The corner building in the commercial heart of town was erected in the late Gothic style and occupied by society's most prominent members. Known as 'poorters' and including the influential Society of the White Bear, they're remembered to this day by the presence of their mascot in an alcove on the left corner of the front façade a serious-looking bear proudly carrying a coat of arms. The construction's unusual but elegant tower is the most striking part of the romantic Jan van Eyck Square and, thus, a fitting headquarters for the city's high-ranking merchants and politicians to hobnob and receive international trading partners. Next door, the step-gabled tollhouse in the same Gothic jacket complemented their operations perfectly.

To end the tour on a gastronomic note without straying from the Gothic path, bistro 't Zwart Huis, a three-minute walk from the Burgher's Lodge, serves escargots du Bourgogne and other hearty dishes behind a 1482 façade in Tournai limestone. The protected monument's banqueting hall is cosily lit, with its original hearths still intact.

When to Visit

Best Times to Visit Bruges

The best time to visit Bruges is the summer, when the weather is mild and the trees are green. Still, the weather year-round is characterized as chilly and damp -- summer temps only reach the 70s. Spring and fall act as shoulder seasons with fewer tourists and cooler temperatures. In the winter, temperatures drop to near freezing levels, which in turn keeps many visitors away.

April-May
The city begins to thaw in April and May, but Bruges has yet to see the inundation of summertime tourists. Visitors will find average temperatures in the 40s and 50s, and the weeping willows beginning to green. Travelers this time of year may even be able to score a deal on their accommodations.

Key Events:

➢ Ronde Van Vlaanderen (April)

➢ Heilig-Bloedprocessie (May or June)

June-August
Bruges experiences its warmest weather between June and August. The average temperature in August is 63 degrees Fahrenheit, and the thermometer rarely makes it up to the

70s. This comfortable weather ushers in popular festivals and droves of travelers.

Key Events:

➢ Heilig-Bloedprocessie (May or June)

➢ Klinkers (Late July-August)

➢ Reiefeest (Every third August)

September-October
In early fall, temperatures begin their descent into the 50s, driving away tourist throngs. If you're willing to do your travel itinerary in layers, this could be a golden season to see Bruges. Plus, hotel prices will dip a little after the summertime high season.

November-March
It's cold and wet this time of year with average lows just above freezing and average highs in the mid 40s. You're sure to find some nice hotel

deals, but you'll be doing your touring in a heavy winter coat.

Getting Around Bruges

The best way to get around Bruges is on foot. The city is small -- in fact, you can walk from one end to the other in 30 minutes. Biking is the second best way to get around. There's also a small bus system, but it's most useful in getting from the train station to the city center rather than for exploring the city. Cars are really not recommended since Bruges' streets are narrow and webbed with canals. You can also get taxis, but you'll have to reserve them in advance rather than hail them from the street. The closest major airport is Brussels International (BRU), so most visitors take the train into Bruges. The train station is located just southeast of the city center, about a 12-minute walk from Minnewater Lake.

On foot: This medieval city is so small that traversing it on foot is the best way to get around. Tourism Bruges offers a handful of walking tour itineraries to help you pack the most sightseeing into your meandering. But please wear some sensible shoes, since the cobblestone streets can be tough on your feet.

Bicycle: Bikes are another great option for getting around. Bruges is very amenable to cyclists with numerous rental shops and designated bike lanes. But watch out for oblivious pedestrians who might unknowingly step in front of your bike.

Bus: De Lijn operates bus services throughout the city and its outskirts. Many tourists use the bus to get from the Bruges train station to the center of town, but since city is so small, you really don't need a bus to maneuver around it. One-way tickets usually cost less than €2 EUR or about $3 USD.

Car: A car is really not recommended for a few reasons: First, Bruges has medieval streets that are narrow and made of cobblestones -- not the best driving terrain. And two, parking is very scarce. Parking rules are also strictly enforced, so you could very well walk away with a costly ticket. If you're driving into the city, you can park your vehicle in a few places: a hotel lot, a handful of underground parking garages or a free parking zone, several of which are located outside of Bruges.

Taxi: You can't hail taxis from the street, so if you want to hitch a ride from your hotel or restaurant, you'll need to call (the numbers are

050 33 44 44 or 050 38 46 60). The only other option is to wait in line for a taxi at the train station on Stationsplein or at Markt.

The End

Lightning Source UK Ltd.
Milton Keynes UK
UKHW020631171120
373555UK00011B/770

9 781715 758691